Pragmatic Fund-Raising for College Administrators and Development Officers

Ralph L. Lowenstein

University Press of Florida

Gainesville Tallahassee Tampa Boca Raton
Pensacola Orlando Miami Jacksonville

Copyright 1997 by the Board of Regents of the State of Florida
Printed in the United States of America on acid-free paper

02 01 00 99 98 97 6 5 4 3 2 1

Library of Congress Cataloging-in-Publication Data
Lowenstein, Ralph Lynn, 1930-
Pragmatic fund-raising for college administrators and development
officers / Ralph L. Lowenstein.
    p. cm.
Includes index.
ISBN 0-8130-1525-1 (alk. paper)
1. Educational fund-raising—United States. 2. Universities and
colleges—United States—Finance. I. Title.
LB2336.L69 1997
378'.00681—dc21 97-15573

The University Press of Florida is the scholarly publishing agency for
the State University System of Florida, comprised of Florida A & M
University, Florida Atlantic University, Florida International University, Florida State University, University of Central Florida, University
of Florida, University of North Florida, University of South Florida,
and University of West Florida.

University Press of Florida
15 Northwest 15th Street
Gainesville, FL 32611

For my dear friends
Marion B. Brechner
and the late
Joseph L. Brechner

Contents

Foreword

Andrew A. Sorensen
President, University of Alabama

At a time when state and federal resources for higher education are shrinking, no objective is more important to public and private universities than the acquisition of funds from nongovernment sources. Although grants—one obvious source of support—are usually initiated by professors and other research staff, fund-raising is the direct responsibility of college administrators and development officers.

For those college administrators new to fund-raising and for those who might wish to consider a different perspective on this increasingly critical activity I recommend a careful reading of this book. It is the outgrowth of a much smaller version that I asked Ralph to write for his fellow University of Florida administrators when I was provost. His fund-raising was so successful, I insisted he share his knowledge and techniques.

Ralph was chair of the News-Editorial Department at University of Missouri's School of Journalism before becoming dean of the College of Journalism and Communications at UF in 1976. At that time the entire University of Florida Foundation, our fund-raising arm, had a professional staff of only three persons. Although that staff subsequently grew to more than 150, Ralph became and for eighteen years remained the principal fund-raiser for his college, earning a national reputation as one of the best fund-raisers in journalism education.

When he assumed his position as dean, his college had less than $2 million in its endowment. When he departed eighteen years later, it had $22 million in cash endowments, pledges, and bequests and was acknowledged as the wealthiest journalism school in the nation. The public radio and television stations Ralph supervised had raised less than $30,000 a year in gifts prior to his arrival. When he departed, they were receiving more than $1 million a year from viewers and business underwriters. Thus, the fact that Ralph was able to practice what he advises in this book is abundantly evident.

To prevent those reading this foreword from concluding that Ralph devoted himself exclusively to fund-raising, I will relate some things about his academic leadership, as well. Ralph headed one of the largest schools of journalism in America, with more than 1,600 students. In addition, he directly supervised one public radio station, two commercial radio stations, one public television station, and one educational television station. During his tenure as dean, each of the four academic disciplines in his college was ranked in the top ten in *every* national survey (nine surveys in all) by academics and professionals. In a 1996 *U.S. News and World Report* survey, three of his college's four graduate programs were ranked in the top two nationwide, while the fourth was ranked in the top six. His university-owned commercial stations paid their own way, and his NPR and PBS stations were always among the top five public stations nationally in percentage of homes listening or viewing. In 1994 the Freedom Forum named him Journalism Administrator of the Year.

Each college administrator and development officer will develop his or her own style in fund-raising, just as each academic unit has different constituents, traditions, problems, and potential. Ralph's advice is intended only to give new and experienced deans, development officers, and other college administrators ideas for improving their fund-raising skills. I am confident any administrator faced with the challenging and vital task of fund-raising will find his suggestions helpful.

Acknowledgments

I would like to thank Andrew A. Sorensen, former provost of the University of Florida and current president of the University of Alabama at Tuscaloosa, for his help and encouragement in the writing of this book. My thanks also go to James L. Terhune, associate dean of the UF College of Journalism and Communications; Helen Aller, former director of the UF College of Journalism and Communications' Knight Scholarship and Placement Center; and Dan Ott, director of Planned Giving for the University of Florida Foundation. Jim is the indefatigable editor of the *communigator,* one of our most important fund-raising tools. For nearly fifteen years, Helen was my collaborator on every grant proposal submitted by the dean's office. Dan gave me invaluable advice for Chapter 8. I was also fortunate enough to have the direct and almost daily assistance during most of my fund-raising career of two outstanding associate vice presidents of the University of Florida Foundation: J. Jeffrey Robison, now president of the Florida State University Foundation, and Paul A. Robell, now vice president for Development and Alumni Affairs at the University of Florida.

My appreciation also goes to Patricia Wickham, who organized my office and my schedule for seventeen years with grace and a sense of humor. Finally, I give my enduring gratitude to my wife and lifetime partner, Bronia, who accompanied me on most of the fund-raising trips, prepared the numerous receptions and dinners, captivated the potential donors, and shared with me the great pleasure of new adventures and new friendships in the world of fund-raising.

Chapter 1

Suddenly You're a Fund-Raiser

To be candid, academe does a very poor job of preparing its practitioners for administration. Here we are, classroom teachers for a good number of years, and suddenly we are sitting behind the desk of the department chair or dean. It's tough to get a handle on the administrative duties. I used to think during my first few years as a dean that if only I had a Ph.D. in accounting I would be much more effective than with my Ph.D. in communications. You quickly realize that the higher-ups not only expect you to develop budgets, but to raise money, as well.

When I began teaching at the University of Texas at El Paso (then Texas Western College) in 1956, I viewed administrators as individuals who spent 100 percent of their time on academic matters—curriculum, faculty tenure and promotion, student discipline, and an occasional complaint from parents. It never entered my mind that such down-to-earth concerns as fund-raising were also part of the job—and I was probably right. In those days there were relatively few gifts to universities—especially public universities—from alumni, foundations, or corporations. Administrators were not expected to spend much time in the arena of philanthropy.

Now move the clock forward two decades. After twenty years as a teacher and one year as department chair I was asked to apply for the journalism college deanship at the University of Florida. The information sheet from UF said the university was interested in someone with administrative experience, teaching experience, research credentials, media experience, and "capability in fund-raising." I knew I had four out of the five qualifications, but what would I ever do when faced with the challenge of fund-raising?

As it turned out, I not only liked fund-raising but ended up spending about 50 percent of my time directly or indirectly involved in that task. If I can put it succinctly, this is why I liked fund-raising: If you had to associate with two types of people, those who give and those who don't give, which would you rather be around? People who contribute to universities—primarily to young people, if you will—are not Scrooges. For the most part they are extremely nice people. Many have become lifelong friends of my wife and me.

On another level, fund-raising is a challenge to the same leadership skills that often bring one into administration in the first place. The benefits to faculty, students, and programs are direct and long-lasting.

This book is based on my firm belief that fund-raising skills can be acquired. It is not a God-given talent that some have and some don't. Successful fund-raising does require some technique; but, more important, it requires persistence, innovation, and risk-taking—just the stuff administrators are made of. Obviously, the technique and modus operandi will change according to the personality of the fund-raiser and the particular needs of the discipline, but there are common principles for those of us engaged in administration and development.

This book is for those administrators and development officers who are down in the trenches, making the initial contacts with potential donors, and observing at close range the benefits of small and large gifts. I hope no one will mind if from this point on I get more informal and refer to the reader as "you." I expect those who read this book to be administrators or development officers, and my advice is aimed at that particular trench.

Fund-raising bears the same relationship to curriculum administration as research does to teaching. When we were solely professors, we wanted to believe that teaching was our most important function. But we knew that good research was more likely than good teaching to enhance our careers. Research was more visible and thus more evident to our supervisors and peers. So it is with fund-raising.

Your success at fund-raising is a reflection of both your personality *and* the worth of your program. It calls attention to your originality, your drive, and your willingness to produce more than the job description requires. In order to directly help you with this task—a task that can do much for your career and your program—I have emphasized the pragmatic aspects of fund-raising. I want to share with you procedures, processes, and even sample letters that you can customize to enhance your own fund-raising talents.

Although I will discuss the effectiveness of a development officer, administrators should approach this task of fund-raising as though they did not have a development officer. In fact, this is the situation in many administrative divisions. I do not want administrators to think of fund-raising as a task that can be shifted to someone else, either in major focus or minor detail. Administrators and development officers should be thinking about how they can utilize my insights and examples within their own discipline, how they can translate their enthusiasm for their own program into donor dollars to make their work more successful.

Frank H. T. Rhodes, former president of Cornell University, has said that a good fund-raiser has two qualities: "a passionate belief" in his or her own program and "an intense interest in people." Note that Dr. Rhodes did *not* say a successful fund-raiser has to be a good-looking Demosthenes. Looks are unimportant (although dress and appearance might be; I will discuss that in Chapter 3), and speech making can be learned.

A few years ago my brother, Murray Lowenstein, a retired furniture retailer in Richmond, Virginia, invited me to hear a speech on stock investing that he had been asked to deliver to a Richmond women's club. Before the speech my brother was visibly nervous. He confessed to me that although he was 66 years old, he had never before given a public speech. He had purchased a book—*Sir Winston Method,* by James C. Humes (William Morrow & Co., 1991)—on how to make a speech, and he had tried to follow the rules in preparing his talk.

I have to admit that this was all somewhat amusing to me, since I had been lecturing or speaking publicly on an almost daily basis for nearly forty years. However, my amusement quickly changed to surprise, then admiration. His speech was a tour de force. He had a passionate interest in the stock market, knew a lot about successful investing, and, following the advice in his book on speech making, effectively communicated his enthusiasm to his audience.

If you are enthusiastic about the work of your department or college, you are the best potential fund-raiser at your university. You are the closest person to the significant components that make up the university: students, faculty, curriculum, research laboratories. Who else knows your program as well as you? Who else can wax as knowledgeably or as enthusiastically about it as you? Who else better knows the needs, can better make the adjustments, and can better see that the object for which the funds are given is accomplished? Just as the salesperson talking with customers on the floor is more effective selling computers than the president of the company (assuming the salesperson knows the product), fund-raising is most effective in a one-on-one relationship.

Today's fund-raisers compete in an environment in which there are almost a million nonprofit organizations, all vying for contributions, grants, and the involvement of volunteers. Private colleges and universities cannot survive without new donors; public colleges and universities can no longer achieve program excellence with public dollars alone. So fund-raising, whether you like it not, is probably your most critical function. It is now the administrators and development officers who have to raise those dollars.

My tenure as a department chair was so brief that I came to the task of fund-raising just like many of you: ill-prepared. I hope what I learned during my eighteen years as a fund-raising dean will help bring you quickly up to speed.

Chapter 2

Twelve Principles of Pragmatic Fund-Raising

In reviewing my twenty years as an active fund-raiser for my department and college, I tried to boil down that experience to the fewest possible principles to work by. Shuffling and discarding, I came up with those that follow in this chapter. Though not the only advice in this book, these are principles that cut across all academic disciplines; they provide a pocket credo that can be adopted by administrators and development officers at any school. As you will see, the principles are not mutually exclusive.

1. Seek Money Outside Your Home City

It is natural to look first in your own backyard, but the big money is usually somewhere else, unless you work in a major city university. Americans are mobile people, and educated Americans are the most mobile of all. You must seek out alumni, foundations, and corporations in all parts of the United States, and devise means of communicating with them either through letters, alumni publications, or personal visits. Don't take the easy chore of mining the local vein. Work constantly with your university foundation to identify large sources of potential support outside your home perimeter, and be prepared to prospect those sources with pick and shovel.

2. Be Prepared to Travel

A development officer is invaluable in the fund-raising process. But large donors expect to see the dean or another top administrator, along with the development officer, and are bothered when they don't. After all, it is the academic administrator who best knows the needs of his or her program, and can make the best possible case for those needs. Also, a large gift at the department or college level is usually directed to a specific program, and the donor recognizes that it is the head of the program who has the ultimate responsibility for the success of that program. The dean's presence provides extra assurance to the donor that the funds will go to the right place, and that there will be supervision of the program at the dean's level.

Nothing is more uplifting for a donor's ego than to have a dean or development officer visit. You become the donor's friend for life. There is something psychological about this process that metamorphoses the relationship from cold to warm, from impersonal to personal. If the potential donor has a business or industry, ask to be taken on a brief tour. If it's a visit in the home, ask to see the art or the grounds. This will not only break the ice in the relationship, it will enable the donor to see you as a person interested in more than the next contribution. It also enables you to see the donor, now and in the future, within his or her environment, subject to the various surrounding human and environmental influences.

This having been said, I do not want to sell two other factors short. First, you will surely want to get the potential donor to *your* turf as soon as practical, so he or she can get a feel for your program and meet the personnel above and below you in the chain of command. Second, usually a disproportionately high number of loyal supporters of your program reside in your surrounding area, especially if your university is located in a large city. These home-area boosters must be sought out and cultivated. But that is the easy part of the job. Travel is the difficult part, and must be addressed as a high priority.

3. Develop a Personal Relationship with the Donor

Donors are warm, air-breathing human beings. Programs are not. Major donors tend to give to people, not to programs—that is, they give to people in whom they have trust and confidence. In looking over the many large gifts given to my college over a period of almost two decades, I recognized that not one solicited gift was ever granted in a case where the corporate CEO, foundation executive, or individual did not know me personally.

I frequently see administrators send well-developed proposals off to individuals, corporations, or foundations where the dean is not known.

As another Dean (Dizzy) has said, their chances of getting a favorable response are "slim and none." Fund-raising is not an impersonal process. Meals and receptions in the dean's or department chair's home, luncheon and dinner meetings, and attendance at sporting or other entertainment events are just some of the many ways of creating closer ties with the donor.

A university trustee recently criticized a departing president in the *Chronicle of Higher Education* because she "never opened her house up once for fund-raising." Many justifications can be offered (and I have heard most of them) for not inviting a donor into your home. However, the willingness to bring the donor in for a reception, meal, or dessert usually moves your relationship with the donor up to a higher level.

4. Give Serendipity a Helping Hand

You never know where you will meet a donor, or a person who can lead you to a donor; therefore, be as ubiquitous as possible. Your university provides many events where these chance meetings can occur. Take advantage of them.

When I was dean, I tried to attend every university foundation board meeting, alumni gathering, and post-game reception at the president's home. Rather than spending my time at such events speaking to people whom I knew, I always tried to introduce myself to lonely looking individuals or couples I did not know. Frequently I found they had some relationship to either my college or the professions connected to my college. But even if not, the chance meeting served to put a human face on the University of Florida.

I emphasize that you do not have to be an extrovert to do likewise, or even have memorized Dale Carnegie's *How to Win Friends and Influence People*. Brace yourself, stick out your hand, introduce yourself, and talk about what you do. You will *always* get a welcome response, and you will meet some very interesting people.

5. Be Prepared to Say Yes

Giving is not a one-way street, nor is friendship. Donors will frequently ask you for favors (but happily, nothing corrupt or degrading). You are their contact with your university. You may be asked to speak, to judge a contest, to find out the chances of their friend's daughter getting into the freshman class or the law school. I always spoke or judged when asked, even when it was expensive and time consuming to do so. I always went directly to staff in the registrar's office to inquire about an admissions problem, so I could give the donor the details of the problem—quickly—insofar as I could. Contrary to myth, donors seldom ask you to use influence to get an individual admitted. Even in those rare cases where it happens, donors readily understand when you tell them you can't. They want someone on the inside to help cut through the bureaucracy and red tape, usually to get a response and nothing more.

I was the bearer of good news to the donor far more often than not. Picture, if you will, the following scene: The donor calls up a friend and tells him or her that the friend's child will be admitted to the university. In simply passing this information on to the donor and allowing the donor to be the bearer of good news, you have given the donor a gift not soon forgotten.

6. Know When to Say No

The objective of fund-raising is not simply to attract funds but to attract funds that will enhance the goals of your program. Occasionally you or your faculty will be offered large sums that promote the interests or goals of the donor but do nothing but spin the wheels of your program. Be ready to say no in those situations. You should, of course, try to shift the donor to a program related to your college's long-term benefit. If this is not possible, have the courage to say a firm no, even in the face of other pressures (from the president of your university, for instance).

Any new program or major endowment will ultimately cause some drain on your administrative time. Do not give away that time for a program of no significant benefit to your college. An individual once offered to establish a $3 million endowment (the largest cash gift I had ever encountered) to establish an awards program. The program had what I considered to be a negative focus that would not reflect well on my school, and the prospective donor wanted inordinate continuing control over the program. I could not get him to change either the focus or his involvement, so the money went to another institution. I still consider my decision to refuse the gift under those circumstances one of my better decisions as dean.

7. Cultivate

Major donations are harvested in their own good time. I cultivated one major donor for ten years before he gave anything. His first gift was $25,000; then, shortly thereafter, he gave more than $1 million. I counted this man and his wife among our closest friends and would have done so even if they had never given a penny. If you are genuine, the friendship is genuine, even if there is never a cash response.

It is your job to make friends for your program and your university. It might be your successor's job to reap the benefit of that friendship. Certainly, I inherited generous friends that had been cultivated by my predecessors, and I was always grateful for their effort. I hope I bequeathed the same to my successor. The word *cultivation* itself sounds too crass to be associated with fund-raising, for unlike a crop being readied for harvest, donor and fund-raiser are building a symbiotic relationship that ultimately will be beneficial to both, even if nothing more than simple, warm friendship is the final product.

8. Don't Be Afraid to Ask

Timidity is the one cardinal sin in fund-raising. Just as there is a time to cultivate, there is also a time to ask, and it is better to ask sooner than later.

Wealthy donors are asked frequently. Take my word for it, they know how to say no, and they are not offended by the question. Corporations and foundations usually budget a certain amount to give away each year. It's better for your program to get a share of that money than for it to go elsewhere. As a woman in my hometown used to say, "From asking and from getting, you never get poorer." What a great university fund-raiser she would have made!

Life does not advance according to the fund-raiser's clock. On one occasion we had been told that a wealthy individual was interested in underwriting a $100,000 program at my college. Feeling no sense of urgency, we took our time drawing up the papers and approached the individual in an indirect fashion. This man died with his attorney standing outside his bedroom door with our unsigned proposal in hand. In another, more fortuitous, case (some years later, I might add), an attorney called to say that her terminally ill client might be interested in leaving the bulk of his estate to scholarships in our field. In two hours we faxed a proposal to the attorney. The man signed the resultant codicil to his will the day before he died.

9. Maintain a List of Needs

You should always keep a short list of the primary needs of your program, with specific costs, and a separate wish list of major programs that will enhance the reputation or academic life of your college. This will enable you to react quickly and in the right direction when faced with the opportunity for a major gift.

10. Go for Endowments

Endowments are better than pass-through cash, even though the latter might be larger initially. Endowments keep on giving, and they bond the donor permanently to your department or college, usually through named programs, professorships, scholarships, or fellowships. Whenever possible, I encouraged donors to make long-term commitments to an endowment program, even though the initial cash return to the college was smaller.

Several corporations gave my college substantial funds for scholarships each year. A number of others contributed over a period of years toward establishing significant scholarship endowments. While the former provided a larger sum of money for scholarships on a yearly basis, we were never certain if the money would be forthcoming in successive years. Thus it was not a good recruiting tool. With endowed scholarships, we could offer promising students two-year or even four-year scholarships. In fact, during a period of economic downturn, the annual scholarships stopped or were drastically reduced, whereas the endowed scholarships increased in value with the normal growth of the university investment pool.

11. Remember: The Rich Get Richer

Just as banks always want to lend money to applicants who don't need the money, donors want to give to programs with strengths, not weaknesses. Which university in America gets more contributions each year than any other? Harvard, of course, with an endowment of more than $8 billion. Donors want to go with winners, not losers. They want colleges that already have substantial support, not colleges with no support—in other words, with colleges that don't *need* the money. In most cases, donors are interested in programs that will enhance the donor's name as a result of the gift. Thus, I advise you to emphasize existing strengths and existing support rather than your program's weaknesses.

12. Treat Your University Administration Like a Rich Donor

I gave out this advice as part of a speech to my fellow college administrators at an educational convention years ago. Later a number of colleagues told me that this was the main thing they remembered from my speech, and yet it seemed so obvious to me when I was preparing the talk that I almost failed to mention it.

It occurred to me in my first years as a fund-raiser that I was killing myself trying to raise a few thousand dollars from alumni and professionals when at the stroke of a pen the provost could send bucks many times greater my way. At the same time it occurred to me that my college would be better off if I considered the president, provost, vice provost, and vice president for business affairs as wealthy potential donors, rather than simply my administrative superiors.

This did not mean that I groveled before them (a good fund-raiser never does that with a wealthy donor). It meant that I communicated frequently with them, letting them know about the strengths of specific programs and how those programs could be enhanced through special appropriations. University administrators are also more willing to match or supplement private gifts with university money if they are familiar with the quality of individual programs and those programs' potential for increasing the prestige of the university.

In every sense, university administrators are potentially wealthy "donors." There is not one of the preceding principles, excepting the first principle, that I did not apply to them, and I did so continually. I believe my efforts bore fruit.

Chapter 3

The Team and Tools for Effective Fund-Raising

Before you begin the important job of fund-raising, you need to conduct a thorough inventory of the resource tools at your disposal. It's your job to understand how these services work and how you can use them to benefit your program.

The Development Officer

This book assumes that many colleges and most departments or centers will not have development officers specifically assigned to them. If you are a development officer, everything applicable to administrators should be equally useful to you.

Because they can concentrate fully on fund-raising, development officers can be of tremendous aid to the college, as no other college administrator can. They usually have professional expertise in fund-raising that a new administrator cannot match. In addition, development officers can engage in long-range planning, maintain contact with other fund-raising units on campus, oversee production of brochures and alumni publications, and make forays on their own to target alumni, foundations, and corporations.

Development officers might seem expensive at first blush, for they usually cost the college or university foundation from $100,000 to $150,000 a year in salaries (including secretarial) and expenses; however, good development officers should bring in $1 million a year in gifts, grants, pledges, and bequests, making the expenditure for a good officer money well spent. Some colleges are unable to come up with that sort of initial outlay. In fact, university foundations normally pay all or part of the salary of the development officer. But if it's he college that must pay, the dean should understand that expending unrestricted funds to pay for a development officer does not necessarily mean the return of $1 million a year in unrestricted funds. Although unrestricted money usually must be tapped for the development officer's salary, the return is likely to be largely in restricted grants, scholarships, and other projects. The development officer should thus be seen as a very good long-range investment for the college.

Even the best development officer is no substitute for the college administrator, and this burden should not be placed on him or her. Geoffrey Stone, provost of the University of Chicago, described it this way: "A dean is more likely to be compelling" in encouraging a gift "than would be a development officer."

Leighton E. Cluff, former president of the Robert Wood Johnson Foundation, said his office was always open to deans, department chairs, and faculty members—but never to development officers unless they were accompanied by an administrator or faculty member. "Deans and faculty know precisely what is happening in their academic field, and can discuss this intelligently in relation to their proposal. Development officers cannot be expected to provide this same sort of information in a foundation interview, and thus such meetings with them alone often proved to be a waste not only of my time, but of theirs, as well." It was my observation that individual donors wanted to deal directly with and effect a personal relationship with a dean or program head. Thus, the development officer works best as a valued assistant, or at least should seem to be, as far as donors are concerned. They should not appear to be a separate entity within the college structure.

Development officers can play a particularly valuable role in encouraging faculty participation in fund-raising. They have the time to work with faculty in developing specific proposals. At the same time, their exclusive identification with fund-raising helps focus faculty attention in that direction.

The University Foundation

Most universities have fund-raising arms, usually called "foundations" or "development offices." They are generally separate from the university financial structure, although they are still responsible to the university president. They operate within applicable state and federal regulations to attract and invest private gifts.

If you see the university foundation as the enemy, you already have a disadvantage in effective fund-raising. The university foundation should be your most important partner. In the military, tanks cannot run and planes cannot fly without proper support services (the personnel in such services usually outnumber tank and aircraft crews ten to one). By the same token, effective fund-raising requires continual liaison with and support from the university foundation. Here are some of the major elements and functions of the typical foundation:

Foundation Executives

The top person in a university foundation is usually a vice president for development and alumni affairs, and he or she is assisted by associate vice presidents. Whatever their titles, these executives operate at the highest levels of university governance. Because their function is so important to the finances of the modern university, these executives undoubtedly have the president's ear. They also understand how important it is for you to succeed in fund-raising; your success makes them look better to their superiors.

If you are an administrator, don't expect your development officer to be your only means of communication with the university foundation. Try to cultivate personally at least one executive at the foundation. A friendly executive at the foundation can help you see the larger picture of university fund-raising objectives. He or she can cut through red tape, put you on line quickly with potential donors, and relay your own development needs to the provost and president, if necessary.

Specialized Officers

University foundations have staff members with training or experience in specific fields or with responsibility for specific venues. These fields or venues include corporate giving (knowledge of corporations and their giving arms), annual gifts (phonathons and annual giving—usually smaller but more numerous gifts), planned giving (annuities, trusts, bequests), research, alumni, accounting, and legal.

Research Department

Hidden deep in the innards of most foundations, like the rare book collection in the university library, is the research department. Find out who runs this place and what it can do for you. Do you want the names of alumni who are working for companies that match employee gifts? What about private and corporate foundations that might be interested in your new project? Can you use a list of donors who have given your program at least $500 during the last three years? The research department can usually dig up the answers, saving you huge amounts of time.

Reports

I usually read avidly whatever my foundation produced, whether annual reports, minutes of the board of directors, or comparative performances of the foundation's investment counselors. My favorite reading, which some deans overlook, was the weekly or monthly report of contributions from alumni and friends to the various funds in my college. Monitoring such a list will let you know which departments and centers in the college are doing an especially good job raising funds, which donors may be ripe for a larger proposal, whether an expected matching gift has come in, and, occasionally, whether a gift has gone to the wrong account.

The "Clearing" Process

Without a traffic cop, fund-raising at a university would be chaotic. The university foundation can tell you whether a potential donor is already being approached by another college and can prevent another college from approaching a corporation or foundation that belongs within your purview. The rule to follow here is: approach a major donor only after receiving clearance from your university foundation.

Know Details of University Policy

Some universities make it easy for deans and other administrators to pursue private gifts. Others make it difficult. Before tackling a job that requires significant amounts of fund-raising time, you should know the relevant policies.

For example, some universities shackle school administrators in a very short-sighted manner, laying out grandiose plans for fund-raising that target alumni—including those from your school—for unrestricted gifts to the university, not to the individual colleges. Deans are then warned to keep hands off. Other universities allow large gifts to go to specific colleges but take huge cuts for the university's unrestricted fund. These policies and similar ones discourage lower-level administrators from the pursuit of funds. They also turn off donors, who prefer for the most part to give to the departments or schools from which they graduated. These donors do not turn a blind eye to where very large chunks of their money are going.

I was fortunate enough to spend most of my career at a university that had an enlightened fund-raising policy. Except for those donors who had been specifically earmarked and approached by the central development office, deans were encouraged to seek out and approach appropriate alumni and corporations. Any gifts so obtained went into the college accounts, with the dean controlling expenditures. Within my college we followed similar policies. If department chairs attracted gifts, the whole of these gifts went to benefit their department.

Overall, this laissez-faire policy encouraged an entrepreneurial spirit in fund-raising at the University of Florida, with deans working as a team at one level and department chairs and center directors operating in a cooperative manner at another. It was not unusual at the University of Florida for one dean to work in concert with another dean on a fund-raising project that would benefit one college only.

Here are the basic policy questions that will affect you directly at the college administration level:

1. What are the ground rules for approaching potential donors?

Ideally, you should be able to approach anyone after first clearing the name with the foundation. It's obviously unproductive to have two deans approach the same person or corporation at the same time. Many foundations have ground rules that automatically assign individuals to the college from which they graduated, and foundations and corporations to the school with which they are associated through general policy or industry grouping.

In practice, however, ground rules do not usually work out this neatly. Suppose an alumnus of your school has a high interest in an area of medical research because of a particular family illness. You must gracefully accept the fact that the very high likelihood of a donation for the medical school takes precedence over the low percentage possibility of a donation for your program. In a case like this, and many others less clearly defined, the university foundation is the final arbiter. Administrators and development officers who cannot live with that kind of authority will have a rocky tenure in fund-raising. You must clear prospects with the university foundation in advance, and you must be willing to live by the university foundation decisions.

2. What is the net to your school from individual gifts?

Most university foundations take a percentage of every incoming gift for overhead. In the gambling industry, this is called *vigorish* (the profit to the middleman for the cost of doing business). Some foundations take a lower percentage from the initial endowment gift than from a pass-through gift. The reason for this is that endowment gifts will continue to earn money for the foundation over the years, while the pass-through gift is likely to earn nothing for the foundation in the long run.

In my experience, only rarely does a donor ever inquire into this policy or question why less is available for a scholarship than the donor contributed that year. In those cases where the donor seeks details of the breakdown, the administrator must explain the policy and its rationale. I always explained to the donor who inquired that, as in any business, there are costs associated with accounting, investing, and other necessary administrative activities. These were the duties of the university foundation, and the support for these functions had to come from somewhere. Most individuals wealthy enough to give you a substantial gift will understand the need for such business processes.

The University of Florida had a policy that made it somewhat less awkward for the school administrator. The foundation's *vigorish* for an endowment gift was taken out of the first year's income from that gift, rather than from the principal itself. Thus, a donor who gave an endowment of $100,000 would not discover shortly after the contribution was made that the principal now stood at only $98,500 ($100,000 minus the 1.5 percent *vigorish*). Rather, the fund's income during the first year would be $3,500, instead of the normal $5,000 (the expected 5 percent return on $100,000).

3. What is the return to your school on invested money?

Most university foundations promise to deliver returns to colleges and departments of 4 to 6 percent on invested endowment funds. (I know of one university that returns a whopping 7.5 percent.) A failure to understand this policy is the greatest source of aggravation to deans, but especially department chairs, who are one level further removed from the entire financial process. I have seen department chairs grouse loudly that, at a time when everyone knew interest rates were twice what they were receiving and the stock market was in a sweating bull period, they were being given an unfair return. School administrators must understand that the university foundation exists to provide long-range service and stability. It is the foundation's duty to protect your school's endowment from heavy swings in the financial market and to provide for steady growth in the principal of your endowments, thereby protecting them as much as possible from the erosion caused by inflation. In fact, most endowments designed to provide full-tuition scholarships ten years ago cannot fulfill that purpose today, since tuition increases have outstripped inflation itself.

College administrators should also be aware that modern foundations have significant overhead costs. When I came to the University of Florida in 1976, the foundation office consisted of only three persons, not counting secretaries. Today it has more than 150 persons, to the distinct advantage of the university's constituent colleges. The salaries and expenses of these personnel must come from *vigorish* and investment income. In addition, the foundation usually has expenses of which the average department chair is unaware. These might include university-wide scholarships and fellowships, presidential receptions and dinners, publications, legal services, consultants, and other devices and events designed to spread a broad net for potential donors.

The average foundation divides investment income into three parts: (1) an annual income to the college for yearly expenditures related to the endowment's purposes, (2) funds to cover the expenses of the foundation itself, and (3) funds returned to the principal of your endowments to help each endowment grow in relation to inflation.

4. What are the policies on entertainment and travel costs?

It takes money to make money. Businesses can be undercapitalized. Fund-raisers can be fundless. If so, their chances of attracting money are reduced. Every good fund-raiser must have an adequate budget for travel and entertainment. I once worked at a university where members of the faculty were asked to take potential donors out to dinner and pay for it out of their own pockets. Department chairs were expected to hold receptions with large guest lists for visiting firemen—with no recompense from the college treasury. You can imagine the level of faculty enthusiasm for such duties.

Most donors can well afford to pay the bill at the finest restaurants. However, the ambiance for fund-raising improves significantly when the dean or department chair can at least honestly fight for the check, or can expect to be repaid, at least in part, for refreshments or catering at an in-home reception. Every university has unrestricted funds that it can allocate for this purpose, and the sensible university will establish a policy to make such funds available. It is embarrassing, if not unproductive, to travel to the donor's city, invite the donor to dinner, and then have to ask or expect the donor to pick up the check. The fund-raiser should always plan to pay the bill, unless either invited to dinner by the donor or beaten by the donor in hand-to-hand combat once the check arrives.

The University of Florida and its foundation had a model attitude on this score. First, a portion of the money that it collected each year for soft drink concession contracts on campus was assigned back to the college for fund-raising purposes. Second, every dean was allowed to use unrestricted money in the college gift coffers for reasonable fund-raising expenses. For example, if a dean or department chair was attending a convention or gathering for the purpose of fund-raising, and non-academic conventioneers' spouses were likely to be present, the administrator was repaid also for expenses of the spouse, including registration.

My wife, Bronia, was a partner in the many social activities associated with fund-raising. Some universities recognize this role for presidential spouses by placing them on the payroll. The least that the university can do at the dean and department level is pay expenses when the spouse undertakes this duty. At the same time, school administrators have to exercise good judgment in regard to the perception of faculty. I always paid all my wife's expenses for out-of-state trips (if she chose to go with me) out of my own pocket, and I never attended a convention outside North America (even if it were a junket for the communication professionals and their spouses and I could have justified it for fund-raising purposes).

Obviously, the expenditure of monies for fund-raising is subject to abuse. We had two safeguards against this at the University of Florida. All such forms from department chairs or center directors for remuneration from gift funds had to be approved first by the dean, and no one else. Then all forms endorsed by the dean went to the academic vice president for approval. If a university is serious about personal solicitation, it must provide a budget at the school level that makes such solicitation possible. I cannot agree with the argument that because administrators receive higher salaries, they should expect a share of their salaries to go for such activities. For one thing, many administrators who have absolutely no fund-raising function also receive a higher salary. For another, it goes against human nature to expect the average person to spend his or her salary in a generous manner for the common good of the college or university—even though there are a number of dedicated individuals, at every university in the nation, who do so.

5. What will the foundation contribute for fund-raising?

There are numerous fund-raising expenses that a college or departmental budget might not be able to bear. These might include the entertainment and travel expenses mentioned above. They could also include the cost of college alumni publications and the cost of a development officer. Some foundations share these costs with the affected unit of the university; some pay them all outright; others will make a loan until the academic unit can generate its own money and pay the foundation back. At the very least you need to make certain that your unit is treated no differently than others on your campus in regard to such support.

6. What matches are available from the state or university?

People who give money are used to investing. They are accustomed to seeing (or at least they expect to see) their money grow. Thus, anything you can do to promise immediate growth in the money they give will probably spur giving. I call this "igniting the match." There is a certain excitement evoked by a gift match that probably reflects the lottery gene living within all of us.

The match might well be something your state offers to encourage large gifts. My state, for example, matched scholarship endowments of $100,000 or more at 50 percent. This unusually good deal permitted me, on numerous occasions, to convince a donor who would normally give an annual scholarship of $2,000 or $3,000 to commit to an endowment of $100,000, payable in $20,000 hunks over five years. The result was a $150,000 endowed scholarship fund.

In some cases the match is provided by the corporation for which your alumnus or alumna works. This ranges from one-for-one matches to the glorious three-for-one matches. A sophisticated university foundation can identify all your alumni who work for such corporations. You can do it on an individual basis by consulting the annual publication *Matching Gift Details: Guidebook to Corporate Matching Gift Programs,* published each year by the Council for Advancement and Support of Education.

Then there is the internal match made by your university, which might promise to put *x* number of dollars into a building, center, or laboratory if a donor will also give the same amount. Finally, there is the possibility of setting up your own match within your college. You have the ability to take unrestricted dollars contributed in small amounts by alumni or generated by unrestricted endowments and establish innovative matches that will encourage giving for specific projects.

The Feedback Factor

Good university foundations establish some formal or informal method of feedback so foundation rules and policy can be regularly reviewed and reconsidered by college administrators. If this is not done at your university, you have recourse through the deans on campus, who have administrative councils through which they can insist that policies be reviewed or an annual feedback session be established.

To use a military comparison, college administrators are on the firing line in terms of fund-raising. The generals in the rear do not always see problems in the same way as front-line soldiers. For purposes of morale, understanding, and effective effort, some sort of feedback mechanism is a necessity.

One example I can offer involves the public broadcasting TV and radio stations assigned directly to my college. We had some 11,000 donors each year, and we discovered that many of the donors objected to giving to the "University of Florida" when they intended to give to public broadcasting (although the stations received all the money in the end). As a result of discussions on the subject, the University of Florida Foundation made an exception in policy, allowing us to have a completely separate development staff for the stations and to raise and acknowledge funds under each station's logo and name rather than those of the University of Florida. I cannot say enough about the benefits of having a university foundation that operates in such a nonbureaucratic fashion. I expect that if deans on other campuses were assertive enough as a group, they could make their foundations more like the University of Florida model.

Internal Organization

No administrator can devote major portions of time to fund-raising (I believe I spent more than 50 percent of my time in this pursuit, directly or indirectly) without effective delegation of other duties normally belonging to the dean or department chair. I was very fortunate in having an associate dean who fully understood this division of labor and was willing to take both the responsibility and the burden that went with this delegation. In delegating, you need to make certain that the authority commensurate with responsibility is also delegated.

Record Keeping

Your university foundation will probably keep excellent records for you. But these records are no substitute for in-office, detailed records, especially on endowment funds and renewable gifts. You should keep a separate file on every such account, with a form that presents a clear record of the donor's wishes and contacts, as well as amounts, dates, and sources of gifts (see Exhibit A). Each annual gift file also should have a reminder date on a visible, outside tab. These files provide quick access for the college administrator and serve as a valuable back-up to files at the university foundation office.

First Impressions

There is no delicate way to put this, but how your building looks, how your office looks, and how you look might well affect your success at fund-raising. Many years ago I was a candidate for the position of department chair at another university, and I traveled to that school for an interview. At a break in one of the interview sessions, I went into a bathroom in the academic building and was disgusted to find the walls festooned with racist and sexual graffiti. The graffiti had obviously been there for months, if not years. At that moment I made up my mind that I was not interested in a job at that university.

Fund-raising consists of a lot of first impressions. Your first impression of a donor is not nearly as important as his or her first impression of you. I suggest that you step outside your building, and then, pretending you are a complete stranger, take a walk through the hallways, faculty offices, and classrooms. This is how a potential donor—knowing nothing about the quality of your programs, faculty, or students—would gain a first impression of your school.

Your physical plant department might have total responsibility for your building, but an administrator who cares about fund-raising will also care about the neatness and maintenance of the school's facility and will stay on the physical plant's back, if necessary, to make that facility presentable. Because I believe faculty rightfully consider it degrading, I never delegated this kind of supervisory duty. For myself, I was not too proud to tackle this chore, for I realized that part of my success in fund-raising depended on it. I will even confess that once or twice a year I would visit my college facility early on a Sunday morning so I could inspect the women's bathrooms and determine if these rooms that I otherwise never saw needed refurbishment or maintenance.

I also advise you to take a fresh look at your inner or outer office. Would it, on first glance, inspire confidence in your sense of organization and efficiency? Inside jokes about an administrator's disorganized desk and office might not be funny or reassuring to a visitor.

Finally, your personal appearance should at least match that of the potential donor you are likely to meet. If you would like to compare your own standard in dress to the relatively rigid standard of a self-described expert in this field, buy the paperback edition of one of John T. Malloy's books with the phrase "dress for success" somewhere in the title.

Chapter 4

Capital Campaign and Advisory Committees

No administrator or development officer can fund raise alone and be completely effective. For advice on fund-raising, nothing is better than an advisory group composed of alumni and friends who already have a reputation for leadership in business or a profession. This kind of help is particularly important during a capital campaign, which takes even more time than you can imagine. I can recall one instance when the deans at our university met so the administration could outline plans for a proposed five-year capital campaign. One dean, who had just come from a major state university, stood up and said, in effect, "Friends, have no illusions. Whatever time you are now spending on fund-raising, double it. That's how much time you'll spend on a capital campaign."

We all laughed nervously. How could we spend *more* time on fundraising than we already were? But he was correct. Capital campaigns take huge gulps of time, with commensurate potential rewards to you and your school or department. In the life of a university, customarily geared for the two-mile run in regard to fund-raising, this is the 100-yard dash. The funding goals that you would normally expect to reach in a decade or more are now compressed into a few years' time. You have to travel faster and lighter in order to accomplish them, and you must have the help of non-academics in this task.

It is this need for help that must be turned to your program's advantage. This is your opportunity to recruit supporters who have heretofore stood on the fringes—to make them partners in an exciting, short-term project in fund-raising. If you share your enthusiasm for the task with them, few will refuse to help you.

The Capital Campaign Committee

A capital campaign committee is organized for the specific purpose of helping the school raise large sums through a combination of tactics: making lead gifts themselves, identifying potential contributors, approaching potential contributors, and serving as a link between the school and potential contributors.

You should be brutally deliberate in forming the capital campaign committee. These people should definitely be "heavy hitters"—people in power or close to the seat of power in some regard. Powerless nice guys, such as favorite alumni or local supporters, will not be a big help in a capital campaign, and their presence among committee members who are not their peers will tend to water down the prestige and effectiveness of the committee itself. When forming a capital campaign committee, you should also consider naming honorary chairs: prestigious supporters who are unlikely to be working committee members but who *are* likely to contribute big or to attract large gifts because of their prestige or position.

Your very first effort should be to suggest gifts from members of the capital campaign committee. In fact, the invitation to serve on the committee should be delivered by you, preferably in person (if that is not possible, then by telephone), with the gentle caveat that those serving on the committee should consider a major gift themselves.

The Advisory Council

Even when a capital campaign is not in progress, every college and department can benefit greatly from the existence of an active advisory council. If it is truly advisory, it should be involved not only in fund-raising but in the overall development of your unit. Advisory councils should be composed of people who identify with the purposes of your program and who have either strong credentials in your professional or academic field or, in the case of a lay person, a proven interest and record of support for your school. Unlike the capital campaign committee members, they need not be persons of wealth, or even the top executives in their companies.

Ideally, you should involve them in the problems of curriculum and finances, honestly seeking their advice about improvements in both areas. The best advisory councils are those that are self-perpetuating, with a strong president, fixed terms of service, and a formal means of selecting new members to replace those whose terms have expired. I strongly advise limiting the terms of service to no more than two three-year terms. You are likely to lose one or two very strong workers by doing so; however, you also will not be left with unproductive members who are automatically reappointed, term after term. The productive people can always be brought back after a one-year hiatus. I would also encourage departments to include in their advisory councils a healthy percentage of non-alumni. It's important for advisory councils to have aggressively fresh points of view in their discussions.

My college had one capital campaign committee for the entire college, and it worked quite well. But we found a college-wide advisory council unsuccessful: each discipline within the college had its own needs and, to be properly served, required the advice of experts in its particular field. Therefore, we formed advisory councils for each of our departments, with most of the councils meeting on campus twice a year. The department chair and the elected head of the advisory council worked out a schedule and agenda well in advance of each meeting. This general exercise, which was entirely the responsibility of the department, allowed department chairs to get their feet wet in the art of fund-raising and to make the social arrangements and personal associations so necessary to the entire effort.

As dean, I made it a point to clear as much of my calendar as possible when an advisory council was to be on campus. I sat in on meetings throughout the day, and my wife and I looked forward to having dinner with council members (and spouses, if they had made the trip) on at least one evening. Over a period of years, this type of bonding between college administrators and members of advisory committees or capital campaign groups became an important factor in our record of successful fund-raising.

Your goal is to see that these support groups identify more strongly with the college's successes and students. As I continue to emphasize, fund-raising is a highly personal endeavor. Alumni and friends of your unit will exert extraordinary effort to help someone they have come to know at the dinner table or at an all-day council meeting. Therefore, it is important for the dean and development officer to make time to sit with the advisory councils, even if they are largely department oriented.

In my case, four advisory council meetings twice a year added up to eight full days and eight evenings of meetings out of my yearly calendar. But the return was significant, both in terms of fund-raising and the establishment of lifelong friendships. Obviously, deans with more than four departments would find it difficult to maintain such an attendance schedule and would have to make the appropriate adjustment.

Arranging the Meeting

A poorly scheduled advisory council or capital campaign committee meeting can be a disaster. Very busy people will feel their time has been wasted, doubt your sense of organization, and lose faith in the program's momentum. This cannot be allowed to occur. Thus, all such meetings must be carefully and tightly scheduled. Over the years I adopted the following guidelines and caveats about supporters' meetings:

· Try to make the meetings no longer than a day and a half, which is the maximum that busy people would like to be away from work or home.

· Schedule the meeting on the first two days of the week (Monday and Tuesday) or, preferably, the last two (Thursday and Friday). Most people would prefer to attend meetings on a work day and be home with their families on the weekend.

· If there is a weekend sporting event, give each member the option of staying over for it, but do not make it an integral part of the program. Some people do not care for sports and do not want to take the extra time to be away from home.

· Check the university calendar to make certain the meeting does not occur on a school holiday. You want them to see students attending class, and you want student and faculty participation in some parts of the agenda.

· Reserve at least one night for a group dinner, with no agenda. This promotes bonding between members of the group as well as between the group and administrators.

· Encourage faculty to attend sessions.

Here is a sample schedule for a one-and-a-half-day advisory or capital campaign committee meeting:

Thursday

Morning: **Early arrivals.** For those who arrive early, offer the option of attending specific classes as observers or participants; work this out in advance with members and faculty.

Noon: **Group luncheon.** Host for the luncheon is either the school or department. Dean or department chair introduces council members, with brief biographies, then gives a talk on the state of college (department), outlining progress made since the last meeting and any special needs and problems. Council president discusses agenda.

2:30 P.M. **Faculty roundtable.** All faculty should be encouraged to attend. Selected faculty offer insights about teaching, research, and service goals of unit. Question and discussion session between faculty members and council members.

4:00 P.M. **Student roundtable.** Selected students engage in roundtable discussion with council members, with specific questions from council president seeking student level of satisfaction with program. Good opportunity to discuss both background and career goals of selected students.

6:00 P.M. **Reception.** Dean or department chair's home.

7:30 P.M. **Dutch dinner.** On campus or at a city restaurant. No agenda.

Friday

8:30 A.M. **Continental breakfast.** Host for the breakfast is either the school or department.

9:30 A.M. **The overall picture at the university.** A university official (president, provost, or vice president) discusses informally the broader needs and problems of the university, fitting the college or department into this context. Open discussion.

11:00 A.M. **Project visit.** The group leaves the conference room to visit a project research site within the school. The project should typify the direction or needs of the unit.

12:30 P.M.   **Lunch with students.** Each council member takes two or three selected students to lunch at a student-oriented restaurant or cafeteria.

2:00 P.M.   **Targeting needs.** In an agenda tightly controlled by council president and dean or department chair, the members discuss specific problem or needs and how they will approach solutions. Members are encouraged to volunteer to take responsibility for specific projects, working with an administrator or development officer.

4:00 P.M.   **Planning next meeting.** In conference with members, council president schedules dates for next meeting. If this is an advisory council meeting, members recommend new council members to replace those whose terms are expiring.

4:30 P.M.   **Meeting adjourns.**

This sample schedule can be customized to fit the individual needs of the school or department. If yours is a professional school, for example, you will encourage an atmosphere of informality if you have a brief round-table in which the council members themselves describe the latest or most interesting project of their firm.

By the time the advisory council or capital campaign committee leaves your campus, its members should have a good feel for your program and its facilities, and they must have received an honest look at both the strengths and needs of your unit. The visit should be aimed at identifying the members with your successes and involving them with your goals.

Other Volunteer Groups

Although capital campaign committees and advisory councils will be your major support in fund-raising, other volunteer groups can help on specific, one-time projects. These include:

Class Agents

A class agent is an individual or a committee from one year's graduating class that approaches other members of that same class by signing an annual fund-raising letter; promoting a special campaign, such as a class scholarship; or manning telephones during annual phonathons. This is an effective manner of raising money, since it creates a direct personal connection between the potential donor and the rather impersonal campaign for funds.

City- or Statewide Alumni Groups

An alumni group organizes through the common bond its members share as alumni of your unit. With the help of your development officer, an alumni group can promote special fund-raising events and projects.

Chapter 5

Identifying the Potential Donor

The ideal donor is generally an elderly wealthy widow or widower who happens to be childless and a graduate of your school. Since that particular combination of identifying features occurs only rarely, you have to be a little more aggressive in your search for potential contributors.

Reporters are not born with a "nose for news." They learn to see possible news stories in events that the average person would see as interesting but dismissible. Fund-raising is also an acquired talent. You must train yourself to look for possible donors in areas others would see as simply the passing parade of life. Here are some places to look:

Alumni

Keep your eye on alumni who fall into these categories:

- **Those who have given larger amounts than average in the annual phonathon or in response to the annual fund-raising letter.** You might set an arbitrary tickler level at, say, $250. If someone will give that much as a result of a rather impersonal contact, think about what that person might do if contacted personally. In any case, you should have your foundation research department see if it can develop more information about such donors.

- **Those who have succeeded.** When you hear that an alumnus or alumna has risen to corporate heights or succeeded financially in some way, get more information about that person and add him or her to your list of possibilities.

· **Those who have an especially warm spot for your program.** You will recognize these people because they volunteer to serve on alumni committees, come back for homecoming, and are often gung ho for athletics. These people are apt to give more than the average person of their means to their old school. One particular alumnus of my school falls in this category. He was a maintenance supervisor for a large grocery chain. Though seemingly not a person of means, he established a significant scholarship endowment with his own yearly contributions and matching funds from his employer.

Parents of Students

You do not expect students to give you a pile of money immediately after they graduate. But their parents are sometimes able to. Many schools have receptions for parents during graduation weekend. Such events provide an opportunity for you to make interesting, and sometimes profitable, contacts. It takes that initial handshake, a friendly conversation about the weather or their child's job prospects, followed by a subtle inquiry about the lines of work in which both parents are engaged.

Visitors to Your School

Sometimes opportunities fall into your net without any initiation on your part. But you have to be able to recognize when this has happened and follow up. For instance, if a faculty member has invited a CEO to speak to her class, take the time to attend the speech, meet the CEO after the class, or take the CEO and the faculty member to lunch. If an alumnus just passing through town wants to see what the new building wing looks like, take the time to give him a personal tour.

If you think these are long shots not worth your time, you will have to readjust your evaluation of statistics. Fund-raising is made up of hard work and planning combined with long-shots and serendipity. My predecessor as dean once invited a retired CEO to speak to a class and was a wonderful host on the day the speaker was here. To our knowledge, the man never visited our campus again. When he died some years later, he left our college a quarter of his estate, an amount reaching almost seven figures.

I spent a good amount of time giving personal tours of our building to visitors. I never counted those tours as wasted. They made me visible to students, staff, and faculty and allowed me to monitor the maintenance of the physical facility. At the very least these tours engendered goodwill for the college, and occasionally they resulted in very big gifts. One alumnus who got such a tour had an embryonic electronic software business. His business later grew by geometric proportions. When approached for a gift by my successor as dean, he gave $600,000 and credited the tour with playing a major role in his decision.

Sports and Special Events

Athletic events and other special occasions attract persons to your campus who would never come for a purely academic purpose. Invite a CEO or a foundation director to see an innovative laboratory project and he or she will probably beg off, claiming some prior commitment. Invite the same person to a seat in the president's box or on the 50-yard line for the game with your university's major rival, and he or she is likely to accept.

Sporting Events

On the night before the game take the potential donors out to dinner. Invite them to meet with faculty or students the following morning, before the game, for a demonstration of an innovative project. If possible, sit with them during the game. Of course, these are people you have invited specially for this event. But you can make use of sporting events in another way, to meet those who have come on their own. Have an open house or luncheon for all alumni before one of the big games. You will attract some interesting people whom you did not know about before.

Reunions

What is so good about reunions? (1) alumni are older and thus probably have more money; (2) the attendees have a warm spot for your program, otherwise they would not be returning for the reunion; and (3) you can spend a lot of time with the attendees, meeting and visiting with them on a one-to-one basis. You don't need to depend on the university-wide reunions. Think of a reunion that might be particular to your school and run it yourself. Some years ago we celebrated the fiftieth anniversary of our campus radio station and invited back all staff members who had worked on the station over the years. An individual who came to that event happened to be president of one of the largest broadcasting groups in the nation, and this was the first contact I had been able to make with the man. A result of that contact was an eventual multi-million-dollar bequest—one of the largest ever received by my university.

Awards and Speeches

People who ordinarily might not visit your campus probably will come if you give them a special award for accomplishment or invite them to speak to an annual dinner or student event. Again, this gives you the opportunity to use that visit as a way of bonding that person to your program.

Educational or Professional

An educational seminar aimed at alumni or professionals can also attract potential donors. In planning such an event, you might send invitations only to those who are high on your approach list because of their professional positions or giving history.

The Proximity Factor

I must refer here back to Chapter 2's first principle, which urged you to get out of your home city to hunt for funds. I commented, however, that a disproportionate number of loyal supporters *do* live in your university city or surrounding area. Why is this so? It's because the people nearest you can see what you do every week or every month. They are committed to your program because it is natural to support those causes closest to home. These prospective supporters could be current or former faculty. They could be business and professional people who want to support a program they can see and touch. They could also be people who would like to be recognized by their peers and neighbors.

We frequently ignore these people, either because they are like the Empire State Building to a New Yorker—a feature seen every day—or like the prophet who is not without honor, save in his own country. Yet these are the very easiest of all potential donors to reach. One simple way to do this is to arrange at least one open house a year in which the people in your city and surrounding community are invited to come to your school and observe a new project, hear a special lecture, or simply get together for a reception. It is easy for these people to join you on such occasions. From that point on it is a matter of identifying those who are most likely to contribute to your program and then dealing with them on a one-to-one basis.

Trade and Professional Publications

Faculty are accustomed to reading academic publications in their own field. Once you become an administrator or development officer, it is imperative that you begin reading the major trade publications in the professional fields associated with your programs. Reading such publications will allow you to speak a common language with the graduates of your school, and they will keep you abreast of developments that will, indirectly, provide fund-raising opportunities. For example:

· The industry has a problem for which it is either seeking a solution or should be seeking a solution. This is a perfect opportunity for you to write the president of an appropriate professional association and suggest your school or department as a site for an experiment or conference (see Exhibit B).

· A graduate of your program has been recognized by an association for an award, or has been elected its president. This is your opportunity to open communications with that individual (see Exhibit C).

Depending on the particular field you represent, it might be difficult for you to shift gears and devote time to reading the sort of publications that will aid you not one bit in the areas of research you have been involved in since graduate school. However, you cannot become an effective fund-raiser without making this effort.

Death and Taxes

Two events over which you have no control present high-percentage opportunities for fund-raising: the death of an alumnus or alumna, and the sale of an expensive property or business.

Death

This is a subject that most of us would prefer not to handle. Even writing about it risks my being compared to an undertaker's assistant. Death, however, is a fact of life, especially for a fund-raiser. So let's talk about it.

As a dean for eighteen years, I learned the hard way that nothing—nothing!—is more important to a faculty or staff member than the presence of the dean at a time of bereavement. Early on, I inadvertently hurt a faculty member by not attending the funeral of a member of his immediate family. Thereafter, whenever a member of my staff had a bereavement, I did not hesitate to get on the telephone or visit a home to offer my condolences, and I never missed a funeral, unless I happened to be out of town. In addition, I always wrote a letter to a faculty or staff member offering condolences on behalf of the college.

If this is important to your faculty—and experience has taught me that it is—imagine the reaction of alumni that you already know. Certainly they would not expect a visit, but they would be pleased and probably comforted if you took the time to telephone them. What do you say to the bereaved? Something simple like this: "Ann, this is _____ from the University of _____. I was sorry to hear about Richard's untimely death, and just wanted to express my condolences to you and the family on behalf of the college. Richard was a valued and loyal alumnus of the college, and I want you to know that if the college can do anything for you, we are ready to assist."

It is not easy for the average person to make a phone call of that nature. But you should see it as a positive way of comforting the family, and possibly even aiding the family in establishing a memorial for the deceased at your school. I never suggested in my personal contact with the family that they set up a memorial scholarship. My presence, however, provided an identification with this possibility. Depending on the circumstances, it would not be untoward for you to suggest this possibility to another relative or friend of the immediate family.

At the time I ended my deanship, we had sixty-three endowed scholarship and fellowship funds, ranging in size from $20,000 to $800,000. Fully one-third of these were memorial scholarships or fellowships established not by wills but immediately after the death of an individual. One was established by the family of a teenager who had hoped to attend our college someday but died in an automobile accident while still in high school. Another was contributed by the family of a corporate executive. Although the family members had a traditional loyalty to a major out-of-state university, they also wanted their father memorialized in the state of Florida, where his corporation was located.

Whether or not you make that phone call, you should also write a letter to the family, and you should do so immediately (see Exhibit D). Again, the presence of that letter might trigger the idea for a memorial scholarship fund, and such scholarships funds are much more likely to be initiated by the family immediately after the death of a loved one than two months or a year later. To be brutally candid, I found that families were much more willing to memorialize a loved one with a substantial commitment while in the immediate stages of grief than later when the grief had subsided. I believe, and often told families, that an endowed scholarship or fellowship is the best possible memorial because it lasts in perpetuity without any maintenance, continuing to help generations of the living. In fact, we would further memorialize the deceased by publishing a short note about him or her in every annual edition of our scholarship brochure (see Chapter 9 and also Exhibit E).

Taxes and the Sale of Property

The person who is about to sell or has just sold a valuable business or piece of property is an excellent target of opportunity, because he or she usually will have to pay a significant portion of the proceeds for federal or state taxes. Depending on the various state and federal tax provisions in effect, that person can give your program a large gift at relatively little actual cost.

When such an opportunity presented itself, I usually phoned the person, whom I already knew, saying in effect, "If you have a tax problem, your friendly dean is ready to help." I would then outline the cost of a project that I thought would be of interest to the person. The follow-up letter (Exhibit F2), which I sent immediately, was brief. The object was to get word to the person's accountant and, subsequently, to get the accountant to phone the tax authority at our university foundation. Another possible approach would be to send a letter first (Exhibit F1) and then follow up with a phone call to receive the person's reaction to your written suggestion.

Chapter 6

Approaching the Potential Donor

For the inexperienced person, approaching a potential donor is probably the most difficult step in the entire process of fund-raising. If you believe and keep in mind that the donor will derive some significant benefit from contributing to your program, you will give yourself a greater incentive to take that first step and at the same time psych yourself up for your face-to-face visit with the potential benefactor.

Preparing for the Approach

Naming Opportunities

Except for the occasional saint, almost everyone has some desire to place a fingernail on the ledge of immortality. At the very least, people are pleased to be recognized for their generosity. Every university has specific rules tying the naming of a scholarship, center, or building to a minimum gift, and this information can be quickly obtained by your development officer. Never underestimate the value to a donor of a named scholarship, professorship, center, building, or room. Even when the project will not bear their own name, donors almost always want it named for a relative or favorite professor. If you are seeking a significant gift, think about the naming possibilities and add that to your presentation of the proposal. In some cases it can make a huge difference in securing a commitment.

Matching Gifts

Many corporations will match employee gifts to universities and other nonprofit institutions. You should know prior to your visit whether such a match is possible. As mentioned in Chapter 3, the corporations that give such matches, along with the various criteria that they apply, can be found in *Matching Gift Details*. This corporate policy can be used to encourage larger gifts from some alumni.

Several of my college alumni with rather modest salaries provided large endowed scholarships as a result of a matching program. One alumnus, for example, worked for a corporation that matched employee gifts three-for-one. In two successive years he gave us $750 toward a $6,000, twenty-year zero coupon bond. His corporation matched it with $2,250 in each of those years, for a total of $4,500. Thus, for a $1,500 gift, he gave us a bond that will mature in 2006 as a $33,000 endowed scholarship in his name. If your state or university has a matching gift program to encourage especially large gifts, you should be prepared to place this into your proposal, as well.

Written Description

You should reduce your suggested proposals to no more than one page in length, with an accompanying budget. This written description is for you, not the potential donor. Preparing such a paper will enable you to tightly organize your thoughts about such a project or projects.

Putting the idea into writing will also force you to come to terms with a realistic budget of costs, which the donor would certainly expect to hear about in your meeting. If your ideas run to equipment upgrades, laboratory remodeling, scholarships, or anything else, outline roughly the component costs, possible matches, and acceptable length of time in which the money can be collected.

When approaching a donor, choose no more than two major projects to present. Make certain that each would appeal to the donor while at the same time enhancing your program. Don't be afraid to dream, as long as the dream has some realistic footing. For example, don't come up with a project that needs space when you don't have space or the promise of space to commit to the project.

Plans and Drawings

If your dream is for a new building or wing, and this dream has some relationship to reality, get an artist to draw a concept picture. You'd be surprised how inexpensive this is, especially if you get an art student or faculty member who wants to pick up a few extra dollars. (And if you're successful in getting the money, don't worry about being tied to the concept drawing. Believe me, the architect for the building will always come up with a design that is totally different.) If your dream is for a new center and you have the space available or committed, get an artist to draw a remodeled doorway to the center, along with a floor plan showing designated room activities.

Brochures and Newsletters

Any information that tells more about your general program should be on hand for presentation to the potential donor. Sometimes a special brochure is created for a particularly large project; this brochure should be given to the potential donor at the time you give the brief oral proposal at the first face-to-face meeting.

Visiting the Individual

There are several ways of getting your foot into the doorway of the potential donor. The best is to have a mutual friend of the potential donor and the university make the appointment. The university foundation should be able to arrange that for you. Another way is to write a letter telling the potential donors that you will be in their city on a certain date and would like to meet them to introduce yourself or to give an update on the progress of your program. I always said in my letter that I knew they were busy, would expect to take no more than fifteen minutes of their time, and would call their secretary for a specific appointment. When I called a few days later, I would refer to the letter and seek an appointment of fifteen minutes.

I discovered over the years that almost anyone will give you fifteen minutes—and I always made certain that I was ready to lift myself out of the chair and start saying good-bye when the time ran out. If the potential donor wants you to stay longer, that's his or her move.

What do you say for starters? There will always be chit-chat about the weather or some topical event related to your university or the community you are visiting. Then you get down to business. Talk about how well things are going with your program, what your students and faculty are accomplishing, and what your near- and long-term goals are for the unit.

That brings you to the point of your meeting, which is how the potential donor can help in the achievement of those goals—in fact, how necessary they will be to the program's future success. You give the highlights of your proposal and budget and, if applicable, show the artist's rendering and floor plan. As will be discussed further, it is imperative that at this meeting you do not present anything to the potential donor in writing. You want to make your presentation as concise as possible because at least two-thirds of your time with the potential donor should be spent *listening*. Keep repeating silently the word *listen* and ask yourself: What is this person's reaction? How interested is she in the proposal? What are his real interests?

Think of this first meeting as a negotiating session. The potential donor is trying to get a feel for your character and the direction of your program. You are trying to understand the depth of her interest, the kind of project that will hit a responsive chord, the resources that she can tap, the time frame for the gift, how you can adapt your proposals to meet her needs, and how and where you should make the follow-up approach. Presenting a proposal in writing defeats all of that—takes the flexibility out of the negotiation.

Obviously, your meeting with the potential donor could be a luncheon or dinner, or a meeting in a home where you are not constrained to fifteen minutes. In such cases, the preliminaries to business can be much more leisurely.

Here are few tips about conducting yourself on the initial interview:

· Don't delay too long in getting down to the business at hand. Get to the point. Wealthy people, successful professionals, and busy executives did not arrive at that elite status by being fools. They know why you are there, and they want to consider the information you bring to them without too many preliminaries.

· Listen carefully to their concerns and interests. This will permit you to customize one of your projects to their needs in your follow-up proposal.

· If possible, and if it seems appropriate, ask to see their industrial plant, grounds, or special collection of whatever. Donors can more closely connect to people who are interested in what they do for a living or as an avocation.

· While waiting for the interview, make conversation with the person's secretary. Remember his or her name. This is the person who will make future appointments for you and perhaps place your follow-up letters or proposals at the top of the stack.

The Follow-Up

In the old days it was always expected that, a few days after a formal dinner, guests would write the hostess thanking her. This rule of etiquette still lives as far as fund-raising is concerned. Within a few days of a visit, always write the potential donor a letter of thanks. This letter normally has one of two themes:

Summing Up an Understanding from the Meeting

If the potential donor has made a commitment or agreed, directly or indirectly, to consider a commitment, this understanding should be spelled out in the follow-up letter (see Exhibit G). If there is any uncertainty about the commitment, you will need to make a telephone call to the donor following his or her receipt of your follow-up letter. Don't be afraid to phone. First, this is far more effective than continual written correspondence: it gives you an opportunity to interact and make adjustments in your written proposal over the phone. Second, although the written proposal is absolutely necessary, a phone conversation adds a human element to what could otherwise become an impersonal transaction.

Inviting the Potential Donor to Your Campus

The purpose of this follow-up letter is to thank the potential donor for seeing you and to invite him or her to visit your campus. Particularly with large proposals, your initial visit to the potential donor does not get you near the commitment stage. It is extremely important to get potential donors and their spouses to visit your turf so they can see the university, your program, and possibly the president or the provost. These visits should be arranged well in advance, through close coordination with the university development staff. For many people, a sports event, homecoming, or special lecture is the kind of event that will attract them to the campus (see Exhibit H). If a commitment is effected during that visit, then you could write the letter described in Exhibit G as a follow-up to the campus visit.

Visiting the Foundation and Corporation

Much of the procedure described above applies equally well to foundations and corporations. After all, they are composed of human beings, despite the impersonal connotation of these categories, and they frequently make decisions based on prejudices, impressions, and individual concerns. If they see your college as human too, you will have a decided advantage in your approach.

Chapter 7

Writing the Proposal

Some people are experienced at writing formal proposals. Others find it the most daunting part of the fund-raising process. It's easier to write a proposal if you remember the following points:

· Foundations, corporations, and individuals prefer that you be brief. Many recommend or require a proposal of no more than eight pages. If you are worried that you have left out detail—don't be. If your brief proposal meets with favor, the granting agency will not hesitate to ask you for detail, if that's what it wants.

· The proposal should be visually pleasing and easy to read.

· Most proposals will be copied and distributed to a screening committee, so do not staple your proposal or put it in a binder from which it cannot be quickly removed. You may place the proposal in the pocket of a folder or use a spring clip to keep the pages together.

   You can complete the writing much more quickly if you follow a similar style for all your proposals. Here are the elements I use:

· **Cover:** A clear but brief statement of the purpose of the proposal. Must stand out visually, listing to whom the proposal is made, the name or names of the proposers, and the date.

· **Table of contents:** A list of headings to be found within the proposal.

- **Summary:** A concise picture, no more than one page in length, of the salient points in your proposal.

- **Background or introduction:** A description of the general problem that needs to be solved.

- **Nature of the project:** A description of the project, including when it will start, when it will end, and how the money will be used to approach or solve the problem outlined in the introduction.

- **Qualifications of your program:** An explanation of why your program is better equipped to tackle this problem successfully than any other program. Usually, this shows that your program is already involved in this particular area or has special expertise available.

- **Budget:** An accounting of what you expect to receive, from all sources, and what you expect to spend in specific categories.

- **Description of your program:** A delineation of the size, breadth of study, facilities, history, and so forth. Keep this brief, no more than one paragraph.

- **Higher supervision:** An accounting of who will provide higher supervision, outside your program. Give evidence that a tax-free entity will control funds.

- **Endowment policy, if applicable:** A description of your endowment policy, focusing on the rate of return on endowments and how endowments are invested and supervised.

- **Conclusion:** A strong but brief argument for granting the proposal.

- **Attachments:** A collection of materials that back up your proposal. If strongly relevant, they may be attached to the proposal within the same folder or spring clip. If merely supportive (brochures, for instance), they should be kept separate from the proposal and placed in a different pocket of a folder or a different clip. Assume that attachments will not be circulated to a screening committee if the proposal is being submitted to a foundation or corporation.

Here is a model proposal, with suggested formats and font selections:

Type Size and Font

Except on the cover, we used Times New Roman font, available on most computers. Except for the cover and the table of contents, we used 12-point type. Even while staying with 12-point Times New Roman in the remainder of the proposal, we achieved an interesting visual presentation by sometimes using bold type and paragraph headings, all capitals, and underlining.

Cover

We used 16-point Arial bold for the top half of the cover page and 14-point Arial light for the remainder. This gave us an easy-to-read block type in all capital letters that would stand out when lying on the donor's desk:

PROPOSAL TO

THE [*foundation name*] FOUNDATION

FOR A

[*name*] PROFESSORSHIP

IN

COMMUNICATIONS TECHNOLOGY

AND

THE DEMOCRATIC PROCESSES

DEPARTMENT OF POLITICAL SCIENCE

COLLEGE OF ARTS AND SCIENCES

UNIVERSITY OF [*name*]

MARCH 1998

Table of Contents ———————————————————————————————➤

The heading is 16-point Times New Roman, bolded and centered. The remainder is 12-point Times New Roman bold.

Table of Contents

Attachments:

1. *Journal of Public Relations* Article

2. *Acme Magazine* Academic Report

3. "[*State name*] State Poll"

4. Curriculum, MA in Political Campaign Management

Summary ———————————————————————➤

Note that the summary, which is intended to provide a one-page over-view of the project, states who is doing the asking, how much money is being sought, for what purpose, and for what compelling reason. If it is a non-endowment proposal, we would also state for what period of time funding is sought. In order to highlight the summary, we presented it in 12-point Times New Roman bold and double spaced. Note that the spacing for the remainder of the proposal is set at one-and-a-half lines to make it more attractive and readable. Double spacing provides less space for the one-page summary, but in the case of a summary, less is always better.

[*Name*] Professorship in Communications Technology and the Democratic Processes

A. Summary

The College of Arts and Sciences, University of [*name*], seeks $1.5 million from the [*foundation name*] Foundation to establish a [*name*] Professorship in Communications Technology and the Democratic Processes. This sum would be matched with $1.2 million from the state of [*name*].

Purpose of the professorship is to bring into perspective for students of political science and other undergraduate majors the relationship between the development of communications technology and participation in political decision making.

This professorship would build upon the significant strength of the Department of Political Science in political polling and political campaign management.

Holders of this professorship would be persons with excellent knowledge about the press and its related technologies, an international reputation for research in this area, and a mind and personality capable of conceptualizing about the future of the media and the democratic processes. It is envisioned that this professorship will give special focus to the new media, such as the Internet and direct satellite delivery, in the context of political decision making.

Background or Introduction ────────────────────────────▶

Now, ignore the summary and consider the following section as the beginning of the proposal. This section introduces the problem your project addresses and outlines what challenges need to be met. Start with a premise with which the reader will agree. Then state the problem as clearly and forcefully as possible. Note that from this point on we are using 12-point Times New Roman regular, spaced at one and a half lines for easier readability.

B. Introduction

Neither the press in America nor political democracy sprang full-blown from the head of Zeus. Each related to the other. Technological developments expanded press ownership and made traditional government licensing more difficult. The proliferation of presses enlarged readership and encouraged literacy, which, in turn, resulted in larger and more intelligent involvement in the political processes.

A strong man with a helper could produce only 200 single-sided folio sheets an hour on the old Washington Press. The first rotary press was not installed in America until 1825, allowing a capacity of 4,000 papers an hour by 1832. This gave rise to the period of the Penny Press and the great expansion of an informed electorate. Each new technological development —the telegraph, the telephone, rotogravure, the Linotype, offset printing, radio, television, computers, satellite communications, to name only a few—changed the way the electorate saw the news of the day. Each development also indirectly changed the way the electorate saw and made decisions about political events.

Political science majors and undergraduates taking political science as an elective course need an introduction to this evolution of technology—how it has affected and continues to affect the environment in which the political parties and voters themselves make decisions. Virtually every scholar who has studied the subject has found an extremely high correlation between press development and democratic elections. This was best stated by sociologist Phillips Cutright, who used a wide range of statistics to measure the complexity of political institutions in the nations of the world. He concluded that "communication and not economic development, urbanization or education best accounts for political development of a nation."

Nature of the Project ————————————————————→

Here we relate precisely and concisely how we would implement the project and what goals we expect to accomplish through this implementation. Normally we would give implementation dates in this section, but our sample proposal does not call for that.

C. Goals of the [*name*] Professorship; Courses Planned

This [*name*] Professorship will seek not only to examine the relationship between the development of communications technology and political democracy but also to track the new communications technologies within this same context. What is the relationship between new delivery systems and participatory democracy? How do they relate to literacy and community involvement? What internal and external controls are exerted on these new systems, affecting interactive participation and access to public information? What new content will work within these new systems to expand the literate and informed public?

The Department of Political Science will appoint to the professorship a person with an international reputation for teaching and research on the effects of media on the political processes. The person would teach at least one undergraduate and one graduate course each semester. His or her major duties would be teaching and research. This will be a tenure-track, nine-month position. The professor will be expected to spend summers consulting with, working in, or conducting research in this field. To this end, a summer stipend is being made available as part of his or her budget. The Department of Political Science envisions designing two new courses in conjunction with the professorship:

"History of Communication Technology and the Political Process": The technological developments that have shaped political information in the United States[, *etc.*]. [*Course description*]

"Using Modern Media in the Democratic Process": As media move from paper and airwaves to pixels and networks[, *etc.*]. [*Course description*]

Qualifications of Your Program ⟶

This section is *not* a description of your program or your university but an outline of your expertise, facilities, and track record in this particular area. In most proposals, more space should be devoted to this category than any other. It is here that you must convince the donor that funds are better spent at your school than any other university.

D. Qualifications for Research in New Area

The University of [*name*] Department of Political Science was the first in the United States to establish a master's program in "Political Campaign Management." It has also been the headquarters of the "[*state name*] State Poll" for the past 15 years, distributing credible information to all media in the state throughout political campaigns.

In conjunction with the "[*state name*] State Poll," the department equipped a separate lab with state-of-the art computer and polling equipment. The *Journal of Political Science* has referred to the department as "the nation's pathfinder in the new area of political campaign management and computer technology."

The Department of Political Science would expect to build upon its experience in polling and political campaign management to pioneer in teaching and scholarly research in the area of modern communication technology and political decision making.

Budget

Unless the potential donor requests otherwise, the budget can be brief. If your proposal is approved, the donor will probably want a more detailed, revised budget. However, you will probably be stuck with the bottom line, so all expenses should be considered carefully. If your proposal calls for a yearly grant rather than a lump-sum endowment, you should list details year-by-year for the duration of the grant.

E. Budget

Income:

Award:	$1,500,000	
State Match:	<u>1,200,000</u>	
	$2,700,000 @ 5% =	$135,000

Expenses:

Professor, 9 months:	$ 75,000
Fringe Benefits, [*name*] Professor:	23,000
Ph.D. Assistant:	12,000
Office Expenses, Travel:	5,000
Summer Stipend, [*name*] Professor:	16,500
Equipment Maintenance, Software:	<u>3,500</u>
Total	$135,000

Description of Your Program ————————————————————→

Try to keep this brief, remembering that your most compelling argument for the grant was in "Qualifications of Your Program," not here.

F. Department of Political Science

The Department of Political Science has 142 undergraduate majors, 58 graduate students, and 23 faculty members, including two "distinguished state research" professors. In the last five annual issues of the "*Acme Magazine* Academic Report," the department was listed as one of the ten best political science departments in America. During the past decade, six professors have held coveted Fulbright Fellowships. Some 3,000 students a year are enrolled in the various courses taught by the department. The College of Arts and Sciences is one of the largest schools in the nation, with 15,000 undergraduates, 3,000 graduate students, and 18 departments.

Higher Supervision ⟶

Donors, especially foundations, will want to know what oversight exists for any funds they contribute and whether a particular program will be considered tax-exempt by the IRS.

G. Supervision

The [*name*] Professor in Communications Technology and the Political Processes would be supervised by the chair of the Department of Political Science, who reports directly to the Dean of the College of Arts and Sciences. Endowment funds would be deposited in the University of [*name*] Foundation, a 501(c)(3) organization that will manage the funds required to fulfill the program outlined above.

Endowment Policy ———————————————————→

If your proposal requests the establishment of an endowment, donors will usually want to know the annual return on their endowed gift and possibly who manages the university's pooled endowments, along with a history of annual returns on investments.

H. University of [*name*] Endowment Policy

The University of [*name*] Foundation receives and manages gifts on behalf of the colleges and other units of the university. Gifts for endowments are managed and placed in a fund where only the income is spent. The funds are held in trust for all units. The average total return for the last three fiscal years was approximately 6.9 percent. Of this, 5 percent went to program expenditures, 1 percent to Foundation overhead, and 0.9 percent to appreciation of principal investment.

Conclusion

The conclusion should recapitulate all main points in the proposal. It should be written as though it is the only thing the donor will remember from the entire document, except the amount of money requested.

I. Conclusion

We believe the [*name*] Professorship in Communications Technology and the Democratic Processes would plow new academic ground in examining the relationship of communications technology to electorate knowledge and political decision making. The professorship would thus make a significant contribution not only to the education of political science majors but to a large number of undergraduate students seeking an interesting and meaningful course as an elective. The results of research conducted in relation to the program will be shared with the public and will provide valuable insight about these changing processes within our political system.

The [*name*] Professor will be able to draw upon the resources of a state-of-the-art polling lab and a cadre of professors experienced in political campaign management.

It is our hope that the University of [*name*] will have the opportunity, through this chair, to develop new coursework and research in a field of vital importance to the political system in the United States.

Cover Letter for Proposal

Once arriving at its destination, your proposal must stand by itself. However, it is always nice to accompany your proposal with a transmittal letter. This gives you an opportunity to add a personal touch to what will otherwise be a rather formal procedure (see Exhibit I).

Chapter 8

Alternatives to Cash Giving

There are many illnesses that a general practitioner can fix, and there are others that must be seen by a specialist. You certainly hope that your regular doctor will recognize the difference between illnesses he or she can handle and those that beg for a specialist.

College administrators are general practitioners. They should be able to handle the negotiations for straight cash giving. They should also be able to recognize opportunities for deferred or noncash gifts, while at the same time understanding that they will be over their heads in drawing up proposals for such gifts. Upon either recognizing these opportunities or receiving an inquiry from a potential donor, I was on the phone immediately with a specialist at our university foundation. And I did not hesitate on occasion to step out of the picture and allow our specialist and the donor's attorney to work out all the details.

Wills

If you are the fund-raiser for your unit, it is difficult to orient yourself in the direction of seeking money through wills. You and your current generation of students and faculty will probably not benefit from such gifts. Nevertheless, it will fall upon you to continue to cultivate such donors, through a mixture of gratitude and fear (that they'll change their wills), and in spite of the likelihood that you will receive no immediate return from such gifts.

If you are reluctant to expend great efforts to get such bequests, ask yourself this: "If I were my successor, would I be happy that a previous administrator had arranged for this bequest?" Every administrator has the responsibility to pursue gifts, wherever they might be. Your college or department will still need new resources after your regime has ended. If you have benefited from just one gift provided through the efforts of your predecessor, you can realize why you have a duty to do the same for your successor.

Indeed, there can even be immediate rewards for these deferred gifts. First, an enlightened university will give you full credit for arranging this gift. Second, these bequests are usually much larger gifts than the person would ever give during his or her lifetime. Third, you have now identified someone who has a significant commitment to your program, and you have an ideal prospect for a current gift.

When persons indicate their desire to provide a bequest, it is well to encourage them to allow your university specialist to work with their attorney. This way the details can be worked out to the advantage of the estate, and the wording of the bequest will fulfill both the desires of the donor and the needs of the university without ambiguity. It is also a good idea to press the donor to give you a copy of the will, or at least pages pertinent to your unit. This permits the university to give proper credit to the donor, especially in the case of a capital campaign. At the same time, people who have put their bequests on file and received public credit for these gifts are much more reluctant to change their minds about these gifts at a later date.

Noncash Gifts

A donor can receive benefits over and above a normal charitable gift tax deduction by giving certain kinds of gifts to the university. These include stamp and coin collections, paintings, books, stocks, land, and buildings. These types of noncash gifts allow the donor to avoid capital gains taxes and to save on eventual estate taxes. By bringing these possibilities to the attention of a potential donor, you will sometimes make it easier for the donor to give, thereby garnering a much larger gift in the bargain. Here again, do not attempt to assess these advantages yourself. Bring in a specialist who can calculate the exact tax savings and explain all the proper procedures, including possible appraisals.

Gifts in Kind

One should never overlook the possibility of a gift in kind, which differs from noncash gifts in this way: A gift in kind represents something that you need for your operation, rather than something that can be converted to cash. The best gifts in kind are equipment, computers, software, and building furnishings. Donors are sometimes in a better position to give you something they produce, in which case you should be prepared to thank them appropriately, possibly through the naming of space or through publicity heralding your program's use of their brand-name product.

Gift Annuities and Charitable Remainder Trusts

Gift annuities and charitable remainder trusts permit donors to have their cake and eat it, too. They can make major gifts to your program yet receive income from these sums during their lifetimes. Charitable gift annuities and trusts can provide returns for donors unparalleled by anything available in private industry. We were able to present one donor with an annuity that paid her double the percentage offered by a private company, plus she received a substantial tax deduction for five years.

These instruments are most advantageous for donors 65 years of age or older who are inclined to make large gifts to the university, especially in their wills, and who own assets they are unlikely to need in their golden years. If their gift is made up of highly appreciated securities, so much more advantageous for them.

By federal law, the donor to a charitable gift annuity can name up to two income beneficiaries. Thus, these charitable gift annuities can be based on payments for life to one person, to two persons, or to two partners and a survivor. The donor to a charitable remainder trust may name multiple income beneficiaries.

Be clear about one thing: Annuities and trusts are irrevocable gifts to the university. Once a gift annuity is made, the university owns the money and simply gives the donor a lifetime income.

With a trust, the assets are controlled by the trustees (which may or may not be the university). The trustees are directed by the trust document to make specific payments from the trust to designated individuals. Upon the donor's death (or the death of those designated to receive payments from the trust, if written that way), the sum contributed reverts to your program for whatever purpose the donor has designated. There are many advantages to the donor, but it might be a long time before your program sees the money. There are two major types of instruments in this category:

Charitable Gift Annuity

The donor contributes a sum to the university and receives a fixed annual dollar amount for the rest of the donor's life. The percentage return is based on the donor's age at the time of the gift. The higher the age, the higher the guaranteed annual income. Upon the donor's death, the residual of the gift annuity reverts to your program for the purposes specified by the donor. Advantage: The donor receives an exact amount each year, whether or not the principal goes up or down in value. Disadvantage: There is no inflation factor. The amount of the return remains exactly the same each year.

Charitable Unitrust

Under this device, the donor's contribution will be placed in a trust where the funds are invested and the donor can receive a prearranged percentage of the sum as it appreciates each year. Upon the donor's death, the residual of the unitrust reverts to your program for the purposes specified by the donor. This irrevocable trust can be managed by your university foundation or by trustees named by the donor. Advantage: As the sum increases through good management, the annual return to the donor increases, since the percentage of return is based on the appreciated sum. Disadvantage: If the market turns sour, the sum can decrease in value, in which case the donor would receive less.

There are numerous other devices available for the same purpose: that of combining an eventual gift to the university with significant tax savings to the donor or the donor's estate. These include charitable lead trusts, insurance, revocable trusts, codicils to wills, totten trusts for bank or brokerage accounts, and life estates on a personal residence or farm. Other devices may be available, depending on the donor's state of residency and his or her particular tax bracket.

A university administrator is neither an accountant nor a tax lawyer. Advice and negotiation about which vehicle to use in a particular case should be left entirely to the experts. The administrator and development officer's job is to determine very roughly the needs of the potential donors. Do they want to establish a lifetime income for themselves or children? Do they want the ability to draw from the principal in case of an emergency? Do they insist on having some input into the investment of the principal? How much do they want to give, and what sort of estate tax protection are they looking for? The answers to these questions can be passed on to the experts at your university foundation. It will give them a head start in providing a choice of devices that can then be taken back to the donors and their accountants or attorneys.

An annuity or trust was never the first thing I proposed to a potential donor, since my program would receive no immediate or near-term benefit. However, for a particular type of person who wanted or needed income from all current capital, or who wanted to provide for certain beneficiaries for a specified period and at the same time reduce estate taxes, these instruments provide enticing possibilities.

Chapter 9

Following Through

Once a gift was received, I always acknowledged it with a letter. Whereas an annual gift from an alumnus might call for a computerized letter (Exhibit J), a very large gift in response to a proposal would warrant a much more specific and personal one (Exhibit K). Do not forget to change the wording of any computerized letter at least once a year; you don't want to send the same letter to the same donor twice.

Depending on the size of your unit, you might also want to determine what size gifts receive a personal letter. I acknowledged each gift of $25 to $200 with the computerized letter, knowing that every gift, no matter how small, would also receive a receipt and an impersonal note from our university foundation. With gifts larger than $200, I tried to write a more personal letter of thanks.

Some departments and colleges have their development officer handle all such correspondence, under the development officer's name. I think this is a mistake. The college and department are identified with their chief administrator, and when a gift is acknowledged by the development officer, the donor gets the message that the chief administrator cannot be bothered with this detail.

Gifts were a primary function of my office. I always tried to remember that the giving of a gift is both a very personal act on the part of an alumnus and a carefully considered, responsible act on the part of a foundation or corporation. Acknowledgment should thus come, or appear to come, from the person who has the supervisory authority over the expenditure of those gifts. Thus, I suggest that correspondence carry the signature of the administrator rather than the development officer, even if it is, in fact, written by the development officer. I recognize the worth of a good development officer, but in written communications the development officer should be to the college administrator as the speech writer is to the chief executive officer—his or her alter ego. A letter can always be "copied" to the development officer if you want the donor to know that the development officer is familiar with the situation.

I also offer this word of advice: Acknowledge gifts immediately. Have you ever sent a birthday, wedding, or anniversary gift to a niece or nephew and waited months for a response? Donors to your unit are the aunt or uncle in this case, and they appreciate hearing right away.

Of course, most gifts—especially those generated by phonathons or annual letters—do not come directly to the college administrator's office. Most university foundations send deans a weekly report listing all contributions received. If the gift was for the college or a scholarship fund, I sent out one of the two letters mentioned above, taking the opportunity to give the donor the latest news about the college and a description of how the gift would be used. If the gift was specified for a department or center, I expected the department chair or center director to acknowledge the gift with his or her own letter.

These gifts, even the rather small ones, gave us an unusual opportunity to communicate directly with interested alumni and friends and to help assure repeated gifts in the future. And they can pay off in unexpected ways. I once received a call from a corporate executive's widow. She was going through his papers and found a letter from me thanking her husband for a $50 gift. That letter was the genesis for a $300,000 scholarship endowment she established in his memory.

Letters of Thanks from Students

Alumni and friends like to contribute to scholarship funds because the funds usually carry a name with which they can identify and are directed at helping students as individuals. In the case of scholarships provided by an individual (as opposed to scholarships established by a foundation gift), my college had a policy of not giving the first scholarship check to any student unless the student first showed us a copy of his or her letter of thanks to the donor. The student was expected to tell the donor a little about his or her professional aspirations.

Donors, of course, thought these letters were spontaneous and were very impressed by the upbringing of the students whom we were attracting to the college. In addition to the student's letter, our scholarship director wrote each year to every major scholarship donor, giving a brief biography of the student who had been awarded that specific scholarship (Exhibit L).

Keeping the Faculty Informed

It is a good idea to keep faculty informed about fund-raising priorities. This can be done at faculty meetings and via internal newsletters. Usually, faculty provide the closest contacts with alumni. Fund-raising is not a high priority with faculty, but if they are constantly aware of the benefits of fund-raising to the college, they will pass on the names of prospects as a matter of course. One $2 million bequest to our college was a direct result of a faculty member's tip to me that an alumnus was ripe for an approach.

Communicating

You are here. Donors are there. Good fund-raisers have to establish some system that permits regular communication with small and large donors. Here are a few ideas and methods that can save an administrator or development officer time:

Using a Computer

What would have seemed an incredible amount of paperwork as little as ten years ago is today reduced and simplified by the proper and systematic use of computers. It might surprise you to know that I handled virtually all correspondence with major donors and potential donors myself. I had on my hard drive all addresses of donors, along with the salutation, and several sample letters. I could easily customize any form letter with personal references, then print it on the laser printer next to my computer. Minimal word processing skills combined with a first-rate computer and printer will enable any college administrator to produce large amounts of customized material quickly.

Scholarship and Gift Brochures

The most effective tool in my correspondence with donors was a very simple, inexpensive scholarship brochure (Exhibit E) that listed not only all scholarships but all endowments in the college itself. In every proposal for an annual scholarship or scholarship endowment, and in almost any other kind of proposal, I enclosed a copy of this brochure. It showed the very broad support we had for our program and the purposes for which the scholarships and other major gifts were directed.

Although this brochure was begun as an information source for our students seeking scholarships, we quickly discovered that it had equal value as a fund-raising tool. Most important for fund-raising purposes, it showed potential donors how *they* would be honored on a continual, annual basis if they gave a major gift to the college. Thus, we not only listed the name of the scholarship and the amount of money available each year but included a brief note about the honoree and the name of the donor. Here's a typical entry:

$3,000 John Tipton Memorial Scholarship

For juniors and seniors majoring in Telecommunication. Provided in memory of John Tipton, a broadcasting executive who was student manager of WRUF-AM while at the University of Florida. Contributed by his widow, Martha V. Tipton, and his daughters, Agnes Williams and Judith Morrison.

We maintained all copy for this scholarship and gift brochure on our own computer and simply updated it each year for the new printing. Yes, these listings take up a little more space, but the dividends are large. We soon discovered that this brochure was a good place to embed nonscholarship endowments as well, so we added the section "Program Endowments," with this typical listing:

Steel Media Access Fund

Friends and associates of the late William C. Steel, partner in the Florida law firm Steel, Hector & Davis, contributed $50,000 in his honor to support media access activities of the Brechner Center for Freedom of Information.

The ego factor in gift giving cannot be denied. One can name rooms and buildings for the really big donors. But what about donors at a lower level? They deserve recognition too, and we were able to accomplish this in our scholarship brochure. The brochure thus served multiple purposes—informing current students, honoring previous donors, encouraging future donors—all at a publishing cost of under $1,000 a year.

Alumni Publications

Perhaps the most unsuccessful fund-raising device of the average college is its alumni publication. I see dozens each month, and few, in my opinion, make for interesting reading. These publications usually

- are graphically unattractive;
- are cold and impersonal;
- showcase the accomplishments of the faculty;
- concentrate on awards students have won;
- contain articles that are too long;
- include photographs that are unimaginative and stilted.

Thanks to my associate dean, Jim Terhune, my college was able to produce twice a year what was considered the best alumni publication in journalism education. What made the *communigator* (Exhibit P) so successful? Basically, it concentrated on alumni—after all, it was an alumni publication. Before deciding on a story or photograph, Jim always asked, "Will alumni find this interesting?"

Each issue had profiles and features on successful alumni; on alumni of importance in a particular city or section of the country; on alumni who had done something especially nice for the college; on alumni who had some interesting nonprofessional avocation, hobby, or experience; and on alumni who had just received a significant promotion or recognition. Jim made an effort to get good photos to accompany the articles and to build up a file of photos and clippings on alumni. He included nostalgia articles about the early days of the college.

Perhaps most important, Jim devoted a large part of the *communigator* to a listing of items sent in by alumni about their latest moves, promotions, marriages, children, and new businesses. These were arranged by academic departments and years of graduation in chronological sequence. Thus, this section of the *communigator* became a semi-annual bulletin board on which alumni could exchange news with each other. To encourage this, each edition of the *communigator* included a coupon that alumni could fill out with the latest news about themselves and send in for the next issue.

The *communigator* was nothing less than a phenomenon. When the University of Florida began a capital campaign in the 1980s, the consulting public relations firm cited the *communigator* as one of the few publications produced by the university that was truly excellent. When alumni moved, one of the first things they did was notify us of the change of address; they did not want to miss the next issue of the *communigator.*

We also put potential donors and key executives in the professions related to our college on our mailing list and sent the *communigator* to other colleges and departments in our academic field. I know that was effective, because over the years we watched *their* alumni publications begin to look more and more like the *communigator.*

We were not ashamed to spend money on the *communigator:* we knew it was one of the best fund-raising tools we had. The twenty-page publication, which was sent to about 16,000 alumni and friends twice a year, cost us under $30,000 a year (Jim pays about $3,500 a year for students who work under his guidance and $25,000 a year for printing and mailing), a relatively small amount when compared to the return.

Colleges must be willing to spend money generously on a first-rate alumni publication. It can accomplish the important goal of bonding alumni to the college and department and can inform friends and potential donors about the college's programs and alumni accomplishments. When I approached alumni for support, I knew instinctively when they had been prepped by the *communigator.* When approaching potential donors, I always gave them the latest copy of the *communigator.* It demonstrated to them that our college was a class act, with outstanding students, achieving alumni, and friends who thought enough about the college and its departments to support both with significant gifts.

At about this point, you are probably saying to yourself, "Sure, the *communigator* is produced by a communications school. It should be good.

But we do not have that kind of expertise." There are very few universities these days that do not have communications programs. Seek their help.

Remembering Those Who Gave

We tend to forget people who have given generously, since we now must turn our attention to the next potential donor. On the other hand, if there is a person who has made a bequest (which he or she could change) or who is a hot prospect for additional gifts, we exercise what is called "stewardship," or the maintenance of contact and cultivation.

It always occurred to me that there is something wrong with this. The person who has given generously, even though he or she might never give again, should not be treated so thoughtlessly. Therefore, I allocated stewardship time to those who had already given, as well as to those who might give in the future. Here are some tools of stewardship:

Phone Calls

The telephone is a wonderful instrument. It's faster to dial than to type an inside address. A phone conversation is very personal, and you are able to get instant feedback about the situation of the donor. Frequently, I would call up a past donor just to say hello. They were always pleasantly surprised that I would be calling without asking them for anything.

Birthdays

For large donors, especially those with whom you have effected a personal relationship, send a short note of birthday greetings. If the donor is a woman, think about sending flowers.

Visits

Whether you are in your own city or traveling, consider having lunch or dinner with a past donor or an alumnus who lives in the area.

Christmas Gifts

Each year, I would try to think of some small, meaningful gift, usually worth under $15, that I could send to the outstanding supporters of our program. In choosing the gift, I always asked: "Will they think of my college when they see this object over the years?" One very nice gift was a book on gems written by Fred Ward, an alumnus of the college and a writer-photographer for the *National Geographic.* I could give a gift and brag about an alumnus at the same time. (For an example of this type of transmittal letter, see Exhibit M2.)

I think the best idea I ever had was for a teak paper clip holder emblazoned with the name of the college. A humorous letter from the dean accompanied the gift (Exhibit M1). Years later people would tell me, "I think of your college every day." They would then laugh and say that the paper clip holder was firmly ensconced on their desk. You cannot begin thinking about the selection of a Christmas gift in December, or even November. If it's to be something special and unique, you must begin planning for it much earlier.

Annual Reminder Letter

I maintained on a computer disk the names and addresses of all major contributors to our endowment funds. In early November of every year, I would give them a report on their particular endowment fund. If they still owed payments on the fund, I reminded them specifically about it so they could plan to send in the payment before the first of the year (Exhibit N). If they had completed the payments, I invited them to make an additional contribution (Exhibit O). This annual letter killed about four birds with one stone. It showed that we were continually accountable for the funds they had already given, served as a reminder of payments due, updated the donor on the progress of the college, and provided an opportunity for me to append a very personal holiday greeting to what was otherwise computer-driven material.

Remembering Those Who Might Give

As a college administrator, you have to shift gears in your reading material—from scholarly journals to anything that will give you news about potential donors. This will include professional industry publications, if you are in a professional school, and any magazines or newsletters that tell you about the goings and comings of the people who might someday be contributors.

When you read about a newly promoted or transferred executive who could play an important part in a proposal at some time in the future, it is well to write a short letter of congratulations, opening the door to a visit from you or an invitation to the potential donor to visit your program. If one assiduously shoots these little arrows into the air, a few will occasionally hit their mark.

When Marion Cartier died in 1995, she left $2.3 million in jewelry and gems to St. Louis University, in a city she had visited only once in her life. She had been cultivated by the Reverend J. Barry McGannon, the university's vice chancellor for development, for eleven years. Later that same year there were remarkable stories about a 101-year-old recluse named Anne Scheiber who left $22 million to Yeshiva University and an 87-year-old Mississippi washerwoman named Oseola McCarty who donated $150,000 for an endowed scholarship for black students at the University of Mississippi. Gifts do not just drop from heaven. Someone pulled a bowstring and sent enough arrows into the air.

I mentioned earlier the acknowledgment of a $50 gift that later resulted in a $300,000 contribution. Another case concerns an elderly woman in a nearby city who watched our university Public Broadcasting Service station and had apparently heard us say quite proudly during our on-air fund-raising drives that we utilized some 200 students each year in our station operations. When she died, she left her entire fortune, almost $300,000, for a scholarship endowment for broadcasting students.

Arrows, arrows, arrows.

Chapter 10

Defeat and Success

College administrators are sometimes characterized by the less-knowledge-able faculty as useless appendages to the academic process—until, that is, the college or the department drifts. Then it is the college administrators who are blamed by the same faculty for not providing adequate wind for the college's sails. The same is true about fund-raising. If it goes well, it's simply a recognition of the quality of the faculty. If it goes poorly, it's because of the indolence or ineptness of the dean and department chairs.

Actually, administrators *are* responsible for the direction and progress of the college, and administrators are also responsible for fund-raising. It goes with the territory. Therefore, modern administrators must expect to allocate a certain portion of every working day to fund-raising, direct and indirect. While aiming for success, they must understand that defeat is also part of the process. Allow me to give a few examples from my own experience.

I have mentioned the alumnus who established a $33,000 scholarship endowment with a contribution of $1,500 toward a zero coupon bond. What I did not mention is that while I was mailing the letter of request to him I also sent out a thousand other letters with personal salutations to alumni whose companies made matching gifts, asking them to consider establishing similar scholarships. I thought I would become the zero-coupon-bond king of America. Only four alumni responded positively.

We once exerted great effort to set up a golf tournament at a new, exclusive, championship golf course for the benefit of a scholarship fund. Only one person signed up; embarrassed, we canceled the event.

The best proposal I ever wrote (in my humble opinion) gained me nothing but rejection from a foundation that should have been interested in the project, since (again, in my opinion) it would have resulted in innovative, inexpensive, practical research for the benefit of the entire industry that the foundation represented.

I have been kept waiting on scheduled appointments in an outer office a humiliating length of time by corporation and foundation executives. Perhaps the most egregious experience in this depressing category occurred when I arrived for a long-scheduled appointment with a former classmate, who was then a vice president of a major broadcasting network. He kept me waiting in an outer office within sight of his desk for 20 minutes while he spent time on the phone, first discussing dinner arrangements with his wife and then bantering with his son.

Another broadcasting executive attentively watched the network soap operas on three different TV screens the entire time I made a pitch to him for minority scholarship funds. He turned me down cold, then hired the first two minority students the program—supported by other broadcasters—produced.

I recount these incidents in this final chapter of the book because I want to emphasize that fund-raising is a tough, demanding business, with more than its share of defeats for every victory. If you cannot stand rejection, stay out of fund-raising.

As the athletes say, there is no gain without pain. I believe every good development officer knows this already, but in today's environment of university funding, college administrators must be willing to share this pain with their development officers. They cannot simply turn this important job over to the college development officer and let him or her take it from there. The most successful administrators in fund-raising are those who devote huge hunks of time to planning new projects with their development officers, getting involved in the proposal-writing process, and visiting potential donors.

Then there are the countless hours, also a part of fund-raising, that involve writing letters, supervising ledgers, fielding telephone calls, fulfilling requests from donors, reading professional publications, and making travel arrangements. For those hours of hard work you will reap a harvest of successes: scholarships and fellowships that attract bright and deserving students to your programs; professorship endowments that enhance the salaries of the best professors and bring outstanding teachers and scholars to your college; and new buildings and facilities that allow students and researchers to study and work in a state-of-the-art environment. You also have the satisfaction of knowing that you have guided individual donors and foundations toward an area of giving that directly benefits deserving individuals while indirectly benefiting society itself.

There are also very personal rewards that cannot be counted in money or recognition. I think of friendships made along the way and of the continually new discovery that there are a lot of altruistic people out there willing to support your college with time and money. College administrators are their principal links to the academic world they only dimly remember from their undergraduate days, or little understand today.

One corporate executive complained humorously to a friend that I had been pounding on him for years for a contribution. But when he finally gave, it was in the form of a bequest that some day will be one of the largest gifts ever received by my university. He announced the gift with this simple comment: "All that I became in my professional life I owe to the opportunities that I found at the University of Florida."

I get a lump in my throat every time I read that statement, because providing those opportunities is the ultimate goal of every administrator. There is no greater reward than for you to know there is a vast wellspring of support for your university, and all it needs is a little "pounding" to make it flow for the benefit of current and future generations of faculty and students.

Exhibit A
Gift Record

This record sheet is maintained at the front of the folder containing correspondence with the donor. It includes not only the amount contributed but, in the case of an endowment, its actual value on July 1 of each year, as well as the amount being generated for the next year's scholarship or program. Gift record forms can be generated and updated electronically, rather than in this hand-entered format.

Page. No. *1*

Fund Name *Joshua N. Jones Scholarship Fund*

UF Foundation Accts.: Endowment *7189*   Income *7190*

Contact Person: *Joshua N. Jones*
2408 Bradford Drive
Columbia, MO 65201

Phone No: *(573) 882-2615*   College Administrator: *Phillips (Pharmacy)*

Restrictions: *Any Student in School of Pharmacy*

Pledge: $*20,000* Date: *7/16/95* No. Pay.: *5* Remind: *November*

Giving History:

Date	Amount	Total To Date	Pledge Balance	Source	Act. Bal. 6/30		Est. Income	
12/15/95	4,000	4,000	16,000	J.N. Jones	3,950	/96	200	/96
12/20/96	4,000	8,000	12,000	"	8,100	/97	400	/97
12/12/97	4,000	12,000	8,000	"	12,150	/98	600	/98

Notes:

Spouse: Mary V. Jones
J.N. Jones Birthday: Aug. 4, 1950
Jones was honors graduate in class of '74 (MS)
on 1/1/96 was president of Westport Drugs Inc., Columbia, MO
One daughter — Caroline, Freshman in UF College of Health
Related Sciences, 1/1/96
Jones is good friend of Prof. Jim Nichols

(endowment form)

Exhibit B

Letter of Invitation to Professional Association

This letter is aimed at making contact with a group of people who might become supporters of or potential donors to your program. Note that it is not necessary to give all details of a proposed seminar or conference. This letter is simply a foot in the door, giving the association director an opportunity to think about the proposal before receiving a phone call from you the next week.

[*date*]

[*name*]

[*address*]

Dear [*name*]:

I noticed in a recent issue of [*publication name*] that a matter of deep concern to electrical contractors is the failure of municipalities to update codes in such a way as to allow less expensive wiring and electrical connectors. It occurred to me that my college has important supporting information to relay to your association and that this could best be done if you would consider holding a future seminar or conference on this campus.

We have two professors, Dr. [*name*] and Dr. [*name*], who have made a study of this problem on a nationwide basis. In addition, we could give conference attendees a tour of our laboratories in which we are conducting ongoing tests that prove the efficiency and safety of these new wiring products. I have spoken to the dean of our College of Public Administration and we believe our two colleges can produce a one-day or two-day program that will give your members powerful ammunition in this battle to bring electrical codes into the 21st century.

As you know, we have excellent facilities on campus for conferences ranging from 50 to 500 attendees. The campus is centrally located for most of your members, and, quite frankly, we would like to give our alumni and electrical contractors new to the state a chance to see how our faculty and facilities are serving your industry in new and vital ways.

I'll give you a call early next week to discuss with you further the possibility of a conference.

Sincerely yours,

[*name*]

Dean

Exhibit C

Letter to Alumnus Who Has Been Recognized

Letters such as this one provide a simple means for you to establish or maintain contact with a potential supporter or donor for your program. An award or recognition naturally generates your congratulatory letter, which essentially says, "We are here and thinking of you. At some point in the future, we'd like you to think about us."

[*date*]

[*name*]
[*address*]

Dear [*name*]:

   Congratulations on your election as president of
the [*association name*]. I know you're going to do
a great job for the group.
   Your former instructors at the college have
followed with pride your growth in influence and
responsibility. Our present-day students could
learn a lot from the model you have developed.
   When next you are in this area, I hope you will
come by for a visit so we can show you how your
Alma Mater has changed since your days as an undergraduate.
   Good luck in your new duties.

Sincerely yours,

[*name*]
Chair

Exhibit D
Letter of Condolence

A bereaved family will probably never notice the absence of a condolence letter from their loved one's Alma Mater. However, they will certainly notice the presence of one. It is always better in a letter of this sort to mention at least one specific accomplishment of the deceased. A tribute from a dean or department chair has its own intrinsic worth. Occasionally, it will spark the idea for a memorial fund, especially if the letter is sent in a timely fashion (see Chapter 5).

[*date*]

[*name*]
[*address*]

Dear [*name*]:

All of [*name of deceased*]'s friends at the
College of [*name*] were saddened to hear about her
untimely death. [*Name of deceased*] made a significant mark in the [*type of industry*] during her
many years of achievement and service, and we all
know that this is a far better industry today
because of her contributions.

[*Name of deceased*]'s design and initiation of
the annual [*name of campaign*] was a landmark for
the industry and a project for which she will be
long remembered.

Our thoughts are with you at this time. May
[*name of deceased*]'s memory be a blessing to you
and the members of the family.

Sincerely yours,

[*name*]
Dean

Exhibit E
Annual Scholarship Brochure

Shown here are six pages of an annual scholarship brochure. The brochure text can be maintained on computer and updated each year. The brochure not only informs students of available scholarships but re-honors donors of scholarships, fellowships, and program endowments every year. It also shows potential donors how they might be honored. This inexpensive item can be one of the very best tools of a fund-raiser. It must *always* be enclosed when sending letters K2, K3, K4, L, N, and O, and it should accompany letters G and K1 if those refer to a major gift that would be listed in the brochure. The brochure is also a graphic reminder to the donor of the increased cost of obtaining a college education, as indicated by schedules on back cover.

COLLEGE OF JOURNALISM & COMMUNICATIONS

1996-97 UNDERGRADUATE SCHOLARSHIPS & ASSISTANTSHIPS

GRADUATE FELLOWSHIPS & ASSISTANTSHIPS

PROGRAM ENDOWMENTS

FINANCIAL INFORMATION

**1996-97
Undergraduate
Scholarships &
Assistantships**

**Graduate
Fellowships &
Assistantships**

SCHOLARSHIPS
All stipends are based on need and scholarship, unless otherwise stipulated.

ASSISTANTSHIPS
These stipends are based on scholarship and need, but also require specific duties by students winning the award.

FELLOWSHIPS
These stipends are based on scholarship and may require specific duties by students winning the award.

JUNIOR STANDING
Most scholarships are reserved for students who are juniors or seniors and who have already been admitted to the College.

DURATION OF AWARD
All awards of $500 or more are for the two-semester academic year, usually beginning in the fall term. Half of the listed sum is given each semester. Awards of less than $500 are given in one lump sum at the beginning of the fall semester only. Awards may be discontinued at the end of one semester if grades fall below a 2.8 GPA (on a 4.0 scale). Assistantships may be terminated for unsatisfactory performance. Many of these awards may be renewed for more than one year, but students must re-apply for scholarships each year.

AWARD AMOUNT
In some cases, a student who is receiving state or federal grants will be ineligible to receive the full amount listed on the scholarship they are awarded.

APPLICATIONS
One application form will qualify a student to be considered for any College award listed on pages 3-12 of this brochure. This form may be obtained by writing:

Knight Center for Scholarship, Placement and Multicultural Affairs
2070 Weimer Hall
P.O. Box 118400
Gainesville, FL 32611-8400

1

Exhibit E. Annual Scholarship Brochure (continued)

SCHOLARSHIPS, ALL STUDENTS

$500 ALUMNI SCHOLARSHIP (2).
For all students in the college or for freshmen and sophomores at UF planning to enter the College.

$1,000 BUDDY BAKER MEMORIAL SCHOLARSHIPS (2).
For juniors and seniors majoring in journalism who plan to pursue a career in arts and entertainment reporting or editing. Established in memory of the late G.E. "Buddy" Baker, editor of *Florida Today* and other newspapers in Louisiana and Mississippi. Provided by Sandra R. Baker, publisher and president of *The Times* of Gainesville, Ga., and the Freedom Forum.

$300 RED BARBER RADIO SCHOLARSHIP (1).
For juniors or seniors majoring in telecommunication, with preference to applicants planning to pursue a career in sports broadcasting. Provided by the College in memory of W.L. "Red" Barber, former voice of the Brooklyn Dodgers and New York Yankees and commentator for National Public Radio. A distinguished alumnus of the College, Mr. Barber died in 1992.

$500 PETER BARR ADVERTISING SCHOLARSHIP (1).
For juniors and seniors planning to enter the field of advertising. Provided by Peter C. Barr, a 1957 graduate of the College and partner in the Fry/Hammond/Barr advertising agency of Orlando.

$800 BARRY M. BERISH SCHOLARSHIP (1).
For juniors and seniors majoring in advertising. Provided by Barry M. Berish, president of American Brands and the James Beam Co., and a distinguished alumnus of the College.

$1,000 RUSSELL BRINES MEMORIAL SCHOLARSHIP (1).
For juniors or seniors showing interest in reporting in areas of international politics, foreign affairs or national politics. Contributed by Mrs. Russell Brines in memory of her husband, former Associated Press Far Eastern bureau chief and instructor at the UF College of Journalism and Communications.

21st CENTURY ASSOCIATES

The following alumni have contributed zero coupon bonds that will mature into scholarship funds for the College:

MARK HARRISON	$33,000
ED & CAROLE JOHNSON	33,000
WILLIAM S. PEARCE	33,000
KENNETH B. SCHICK	33,000

BEQUESTS

The following alumni have provided scholarship bequests for the College:

HOMER E. HOOKS	$10,000
FRED P. PETTIJOHN, SR.	25,000

GRADUATE FELLOWSHIPS, ASSISTANTSHIPS

GRADUATE SCHOOL FELLOWSHIPS
M.A. and Ph.D. students in the College of Journalism and Communications may obtain an application from the Graduate Division, 2104 Weimer. Deadline for full consideration of all 1996-97 awards is Feb. 1, 1996. Later applications will be considered as funds remain. See the Graduate Catalog for additional university-wide programs.

$3,800-$7,600 GRADUATE ASSISTANTSHIPS (20).
Awarded to students with teaching or research abilities. Requires 10 to 20 hours of work a week. Maximum of one calendar year of teaching.

BATEMAN FELLOWSHIP (number and amounts varies)
Open to all graduate students with superior academic achievement (3.5 overall GPA or higher).

$9,000-$10,500 BRECHNER EDITORIAL ASSISTANTSHIP (1).
Awarded to a graduate student interested in mass media law. Requires 13 hours of work editing *The Brechner Report.* Preference will be given to doctoral students who have extensive experience reporting the courts for the news media, or who have a legal education and reporting experience. 12 months.

$9,000-$10,500 BRECHNER RESEARCH ASSISTANTSHIP (1).
Awarded to a graduate student specializing in mass media law. Requires 13 hours of work a week in the Brechner Center for Freedom of Information. Preference is given to a) doctoral students and b) master's students who have had legal training. 12 months.

5,000 HERBERT S. DOLGOFF GRADUATE RADIO ASSISTANTSHIP (1).

Awarded to graduate student conducting research in the area of radio news programming or management. Student must work 13 hours a week for the college radio stations WRUF-AM/FM or WUFT-FM. Provided by the family of the late Herbert S. Dolgoff, who owned and operated radio stations WCMQ-AM/FM in Miami from 1972-1986.

$7,500 FORD MOTOR COMPANY PLACEMENT ASSISTANT (1).

Primary duties are to coordinate internship and placement listings, advise students in the Scholarship and Placement Center and track alumni. Minority student preferred. Provided by Ford Motor Co. 12 months.

$1,500 RALPH AND BRONIA LOWENSTEIN FELLOWSHIP (1)

Open to all graduate students. Provided by media, foundations and friends of Dr. and Mrs. Lowenstein. Dr. Lowenstein was dean of the college, 1976-94.

$1,000 NATHANIEL W. PICKARD FELLOWSHIP (1).

Awarded to graduate students planning to pursue a career in political communication. Provided as a memorial by the family and friends of Nate Pickard, who received a master's degree from the College in 1988.

$1,500 CLAUDIA ROSS MEMORIAL FELLOWSHIPS FOR INVESTIGATIVE REPORTING (3).

Awarded to students who show interest and demonstrate promise in investigative reporting. Contributed by Mrs. Adelaide E. Ross in memory of her daughter, killed while serving as a foreign correspondent.

$7,500 ST. PETERSBURG TIMES/JAMES P. KERLIN ASSISTANTSHIP (1).

For a graduate student pursuing studies in communication law or freedom of information. Contributed by the *St. Petersburg Times* and Mrs. Marjorie O. Kerlin, of Jacksonville. James P. Kerlin, Mrs. Kerlin's husband, was an Associated Press photographer for 43 years and a principal photographer of space shots from Cape Canaveral/Cape Kennedy in the early years of that program. Student must work 10 hours a week in the Brechner Center for Freedom of Information.

PROGRAM ENDOWMENTS

BRECHNER FOI ENDOWMENT

The late Joseph L. Brechner, Orlando television executive, gave in his lifetime more than an $1 million for the support of the Joseph L. Brechner Center for Freedom of Information. The endowment provides support for an eminent scholar, fellowships and general support of the center.

13

REFERENCE AREAS FOR ADDITIONAL SCHOLARSHIPS:

Student Financial Affairs
S-103 Criser Hall
University of Florida
Gainesville, FL 32611

1995 Journalism Career and Scholarship Guide.
Write:

The Dow Jones Newspaper Fund, Inc.
P.O. Box 300
Princeton, New Jersey 08540

AVERAGE COST PER YEAR TO UNIVERSITY OF FLORIDA UNDERGRADUATE STUDENTS

The following is an estimate of the expenses for one year (two semesters) for a full-time student.

	Undergraduate On-Campus Florida Resident	Undergraduate Off-Campus Florida Resident
Registration Fees	$1,820	$1,820
Books and Supplies	630	630
Room	1,960	2,730
Food	2,220	2,220
Transportation	470	710
Clothing Maintenance	390	390
Personal/Health Insurance	670	670
Total Budget	$8,160	$9,170

TUITION PER CREDIT HOUR

Course Level	FL Resident	Non-FL Resident
0-4999	60.77	236.44
5000-9999	116.58	388.58
Law courses	130.08	413.40

Exhibit F

Letters Regarding Sale of Major Property

Gift requests following property sales require fast action. If there is a tax benefit to the donor for charitable giving, the potential donor's accountants must look into the possibility quickly, at the very least before the tax year ends. Therefore, the fund-raiser must get on the phone with the potential donor either before or after the actual proposal is made. There is not enough time to let a written proposal languish. The first letter (Exhibit F1) lays out the proposal in brief to prepare the potential donor and his or her accountant for the phone call in which the feasibility of the gift and more details about the project will be discussed. The second letter (Exhibit F2) is a follow-up to an initial phone call in which the project has been briefly mentioned. Both letters are aimed at getting the possibility of a tax saving before the potential donor's accountant and, consequently, encouraging the accountant or the potential donor to call the tax expert at the university foundation.

Exhibit F1
Letter Regarding Sale of a Major Property (send before phone call)

[date]
[name]
[address]

Dear [name]:

Congratulations on the sale of your Freemont shopping center. I know managing that property has been a large part of your life for the last decade. However, I also know that you will find some equally interesting venture in short time.

It occurred to me, [donor's name], that this sale could provide a special bonus for both you and the college. This could be an opportunity for you and the college together to build the planetarium that our faculty and students have so long desired.

Two major donors to the university in the past year discovered that they could make significant gifts to the university at relatively small cost to themselves as a result of the tax consequences of property sales similar to yours. Obviously, only your accountants can tell you whether you could get the same advantages, but I hope you will consider it. [Name] at our university foundation (phone number) will be happy to share with your or your accountant the details about the tax savings in these two gifts.

I'd like to give you a call next week to give you more details about the plans of the Department of Astronomy for a planetarium that would serve the entire population of this northern half of the state—from schoolchildren to seniors. Meanwhile, I hope you will think about the possibility of underwriting a project that will bring the science and spectacle of modern astronomy to the general public in our state.

Sincerely,
[name]
Chair

Exhibit F2
Letter Regarding Sale of Major Property
(send following phone call)

[date]
[name]
[address]

Dear [name]:

   Thanks for giving me the opportunity yesterday to
tell you about the Department of Astronomy's plans
for a 100-seat planetarium.

   The sale of the Freemont shopping center is a
wonderful reward to you for a decade of hard work,
long hours, and entrepreneurial skill. As I mentioned
on the phone, perhaps this sale can provide an additional bonus for both you and the Department of
Astronomy.

   Two major donors in the past year discovered that
they could make significant gifts to the university
at relatively small cost to themselves as a result of
current tax regulations. [Name] at our university
foundation (phone number) would be happy to share
with your accountant the details of the tax savings
regarding these gifts.

   Your long-standing interest in astronomy would be
highlighted by the construction of a 100-seat planetarium bearing your name. I estimate that we could
build it for about $3 million, with $2 million coming
from you and $1 million from a state matching grant.
The Department of Astronomy faculty has always
dreamed about sharing the science and spectacle of
modern astronomy with the entire population of this
northern half of the state—from schoolchildren to
seniors. A [donor's name] Planetarium would fulfill
their dream, and perhaps yours.

Sincerely,
[name]
Chair

Exhibit G
Letter Confirming Understanding Regarding Gift

This letter must contain all the information that will be used in the future for reminders to the donor. This letter also reconfirms the purpose of the gift, enabling the donor to make a change if there is a misunderstanding. Enclose a scholarship brochure in this letter if this is a major gift that would be listed in the brochure.

Exhibit G
Letter to Confirm Understanding Regarding Gift

[*date*]
[*name*]
[*address*]

Dear [*name*]:

I enjoyed having lunch with you last week and was
extremely pleased to hear of your decision to establish
a [*fellowship name*] Fellowship at the college. As I
pointed out, your contributions totaling $100,000 can
be made on the following schedule:

Dec. 1999: $20,000
Dec. 2000: $20,000
Dec. 2001: $20,000
Dec. 2002: $20,000
Dec. 2003: $20,000
            $100,000
Dec. 2004: $[*suggested amount*] match, if any
            $[*total amount*]

I am enclosing a copy of our 1997–98 scholarship
brochure, which will indicate how we will list your
fellowship. Is this wording okay with you?

[*Fellowship name*] FELLOWSHIP. Awarded to a graduate
student majoring in international relations. Provided
by [*donor's name*], a 1958 graduate of the college and
partner in the law firm of [*firm name*], Philadelphia.
Please let me know if you would like any change in this
wording. I will remind you of the 1999 contribution in
November, as you suggested. You have our gratitude,
[*donor's name*], for this marvelous new fellowship.

Sincerely,
[*name*]
Dean

Encl. (college scholarship brochure)

Exhibit H

Letter of Invitation to Visit Campus

Few persons, even alumni, are willing to commit large sums to a program before they have seen the physical facilities and key personnel. An invitation to the campus is aimed at bringing the potential donor into physical contact with the program and top officials of the university.

Exhibit H
Letter of Invitation to Visit Campus

[*date*]
[*name*]
[*address*]

Dear [*name*]:

   Thanks for taking the time out of your busy schedule
to see [*name*] and me last Thursday. I hope I stimu-
lated your interest in the "English/English" project,
which would send our English literature majors to
hometowns of British authors for one semester.

   As we discussed on Thursday, you and [*spouse's name*]
are long overdue for a visit to your Alma Mater. We
are now making plans for our annual Frontiers of
Literature weekend, and I hope we can be hosts to you
and [*spouse's name*]. The weekend, normally attended by
only 20 invited persons, begins with a dinner on
Friday night, March 23, and ends with a dinner at the
President's home on Saturday night. During the day on
Saturday, we have seminars by the best lecturers in
our English department. I enclose the weekend's program.

   While here, you will have an opportunity to meet
President [*name*] and several of the bright young
master's students we have recruited for our English
literature program. You will also get a tour of
the Rare Books Collection, including two of the
Shakespeare portfolios.

   I'll be calling you next week to see if you and
[*spouse's name*] can join us for the weekend. I attended the weekend last year, and can tell you that
it is an unusual and exciting experience.

Sincerely,
[*name*]
Dean

Encl. (weekend's program)

Exhibit I

Letter of Transmittal Accompanying Proposal

A letter of transmittal adds a note of warmth to a proposal sent to a potential donor. It should be brief and is usually based on the points emphasized in the Summary of the proposal. This letter would accompany the model proposal in Chapter 7.

Exhibit I
Letter of Transmittal Accompanying Proposal

[*date*]
[*name*]
[*address*]

Dear [*name*]:

  I am happy to send you this proposal for a [*name*] Professorship in Communications Technology and the Democratic Processes.

  The proposed [*name*] Professorship would build upon the nationally recognized strength of our Department of Political Science in political polling and campaign management. As was so apparent in the conventions of both major parties in the 1996 election, media technology has greatly changed the face and substance of politics in this country. We are anxious to expose our undergraduates to the implications of these changes in political decision making by the electorate. We also believe the proposed [*name*] Professorship would produce important research that could be shared with the general public.

  I want to thank you personally for meeting with me during my recent visit to Chicago. You will note we followed all of your very good suggestions. I'm especially grateful for your observation about the need for annual research in the field. We have placed into the budget a summer research program for the holder of the professorship.

Sincerely yours,

[*name*]
Dean

Encl. (proposal and attachments)

Exhibit J
Letter of Thanks for Small Gift

This letter is changed on July 1 each year. The form is kept on the computer, and pertinent material is filled in by a secretary from information transmitted to you in your university foundation's weekly listing of contributions. Colleges might want to send this letter to donors who contribute above a fixed amount, say $25 or $50, but no more than $200.

Exhibit J
Letter of Thanks for Small Gift

[*date*]

[*name*]
[*address*]

Dear [*name*]:

   Many thanks for your recent gift of $[*amount*] to
[*name of school or college*]. Support such as this
from alumni and friends has allowed us to maintain
the momentum of the school in attracting the best
students from throughout the nation.

   We have earmarked alumni and friends' gifts this
year for scholarships and classroom teaching aids.
You will pleased to hear that last year your
college awarded more scholarships, with more total
money, than any other school of art in America.
Last spring, our students won the coveted "Emelia
Branch Award" for the best collection of portfolios in the National Art Students annual competition.

   Thanks for your continuing support, [*donor's
name*]. You are keeping the wind at our back.

Sincerely,

[*name*]
Director

Exhibit K
Letters of Thanks for Large Gifts

Large gifts call for one of four possible responsive letters:

1. Personal Thanks (Exhibit K1): for a generous one-time gift, usually of a size (say, $200 or more) that calls for a more personal letter than the computerized "Small Gift" letter in Exhibit J.

2. Thanks, with Suggestion to Establish Endowment (Exhibit K2): for a gift of significant size, which implies a potential for a much larger gift. This letter *must* be followed up by a phone call or a personal visit. Send scholarship brochure with this letter.

3. Thanks for Commitment (Exhibit K3): for the donor's commitment to make a large gift to your program. Send scholarship brochure with this letter.

4. Thanks for Payment on Pledge (Exhibit K4): for the initial or successive payment on an endowment or large gift pledge. Send scholarship brochure with this letter.

Exhibit K1
Personal Thanks

[date]
[name]
[address]

Dear [name]:

Many thanks for your gift of $300 to the Department of Special Education.

We have earmarked your gift for books in our Reading Room. At a time when funds for the latest reading material in Special Education are difficult to come by, your gift is a virtual lifeline.

We are grateful for your continued support, [donor's name], and hope that when you are next on campus you will come by to see how we have remodeled the Reading Room in just the past year. If you can come by the Dean's Office, too, I would very much like to meet you and thank you in person.

Sincerely yours,

[name]
Dean

Exhibit K2
Thanks, with Suggestion to Establish Endowment

[date]
[name]
[address]

Dear [name]:

Thank you very much for your gift of $1,000 to the Applied Mathematics Center. In this day of shrinking state and federal funds, your contribution was an unexpected but very welcome note of cheer.

As you have no doubt noticed in the alumni newsletter, the center continues to win national accolades for its ability to translate the theories of the best brains in mathematics into practical technological applications.

It occurred to me that you might want to use your annual contributions to the center to build a special scholarship or facilities fund. This could be accomplished with your same or slightly larger gifts. Such a fund would become a permanent resource of the center, generating income each year for many years to come.

When we receive sums of the size of your last few gifts, I always like to give the donor the option of placing the gifts in an endowed fund, with whatever criteria the donor desires. I will call you next week to give you more details about what I have in mind. I am enclosing our current scholarship/endowment brochure to show you some of the funds that already exist.

Meanwhile, you have our continued gratitude for your generous support.

Sincerely,
[name]
Director

Encl. (college scholarship brochure)

Exhibit K3
Thanks for Commitment

[*date*]

[*name*]
[*address*]

Dear [*name*]:

Thank you very much for your commitment of $250,000 to establish the [*endowment name*] Endowment for Library Technology.

This will be a tremendous boon to our students in Library Science for generations to come. Your endowment will not only allow us to purchase state-of-the-art equipment for our labs each year but will also provide the funds for software and on-line programs.

As we discussed in our correspondence, the first payment of $50,000 will be due by December 31 of this year. I will remind you about this in November of this year and each of the four succeeding years.

I can't tell you how grateful we are for support in this particular area, where it is so difficult to obtain either university or federal funds for the technological changes that seem to occur in geometrical progression each year.

Don't forget that the school has a date with you and Ann for one of the home games in September or October. We will be in touch with you about that in August.

Sincerely yours,

[*name*]
Director

Encl. (college scholarship brochure)

Exhibit K4
Thanks for Payment on Pledge

[*date*]

[*name*]
[*address*]

Dear [*name*]:

   Many thanks for your check for $4,000 for the
[*fund name*] Scholarship Fund.
   This now brings your total contributions to
$12,000, building steadily toward your pledge of
$20,000. The fund produced $400 last year, which
we have awarded to [*student's name*], a sophomore
from San Diego. I enclose a copy of our scholarship brochure, which lists your scholarship on
page 3.
   So far, the Bird Dogs are undefeated in the
current football season (they do not play their
first game until next week).
Come up and see us one of these days, [*donor's
name*].

Sincerely,

[*name*]
Dean

Encl. (college scholarship brochure)

Exhibit L

Annual Letter to Donor Describing Scholarship Recipient

This stewardship letter is aimed at maintaining the donor's continued support and involvement by showing the benefit of the gift and the accountability of the school. Future gifts might or might not arrive as a result of such letters, but this annual report establishes with the donor that your school has a professional operation. This can be a form letter, with only paragraph three and one word (name of the recipient) in paragraph four

[date]

[name]
[address]

Dear [name]:

   This has been a banner scholarship year for us. We received 12 new scholarship endowments, many of which have already begun to generate funds for the coming year.

   These scholarships join the excellent one you initiated three years ago. As tuition and fees go up each year (there has been an 18 percent tuition increase in the last two years alone), scholarships such as yours play an important role in helping us attract and retain the top in the state and nation.

   Winner of the [scholarship name] Scholarship for the 2000–2001 academic year is [student's name]. [Student's name] is a native of Memphis and graduated in 1999 from that city's Jefferson High School, where she was captain of the school's gymnastic team. She will be entering the College of Health-Related Sciences this fall as a physical therapy major. She is working as an intern this summer at the North Memphis Regional Hospital.

   Many thanks for your generous support, [donor's name]. Students like [student's name] probably could not complete school without scholarship help. I believe she has the potential to become an outstanding professional in the physical therapy field.

Sincerely yours,

[name]
Scholarship Director

Encl. (college scholarship brochure)

Exhibit M

Letters to Accompany a Christmas Gift

Think about sending some small gift each year to major contributors to your program. The challenge is to send them something that will either typify the quality of your program or highlight the presence of your program in the eyes of the recipient. The first letter accompanied a paper clip dispenser given one year by the College of Journalism and Communications at the University of Florida. The other is a letter that could accompany a book written by one of your professors or alumni. If the gift is a book, try to choose one that will genuinely interest the donor, and, for the extra touch, try to get it autographed by the author.

[*date*]

[*name*]
[*address*]

Dear [*name*]:

A German Ph.D. candidate, I am told, once wrote his dissertation on the life of a box of 500 paper clips: 167 were recycled for a second use, 49 were tossed into the trash can with the papers to which they were attached, 15 were twisted into odd shapes by nervous administrators and secretaries, 3 were used to punch foreign material out of small holes, etc.

Whatever *you* do with paper clips (and I really don't want to know), the college would like them to start their public life from a classy dispenser suitably marked with the name of you know what. Keep this magnetized dispenser on your office or home desk as a reminder of the good deeds you have done for the college.

Many thanks for your past gifts. We hope you enjoy using ours. All good wishes to you and your family for a very happy holiday season.

Sincerely,

[*name*]
Dean

Encl. (gift)

Exhibit M2
Letter to Accompany a Christmas Gift
(book)

[*date*]

[*name*]
[*address*]

Dear [*name*]:

Enclosed is an autographed copy of [*book title*]
by [*author's name*], a graduate of our college.

We are very proud of [*author's name*]. She par-
layed her background in environmental science
into a job with the Smithsonian Institution. She
now travels throughout the world to record the
flora and fauna in the valleys of endangered
rivers. These travels have taken her to some of
the most beautiful and hostile environments in
every continent.

This book on the rivers of Indonesia, published
this year, is one that I thought you would enjoy.

Here's wishing you and yours a happy holiday
season, with gratitude from all of us for your
support of the college and its programs—and for
helping us to continue to attract and educate
students like you and [*author's name*].

Sincerely yours,

[*name*]
Dean

Encl. (gift)

Exhibit N

Annual Letter Reminding of Pledge Payment Due

This annual letter serves four purposes:

1. Reminder of payment due.

2. Report of status of endowment.

3. Notice that donor is being honored.

4. Holiday greeting.

This can be a form letter, with blanks left for you to fill in the name of the scholarship and the payments on the endowment or major gift pledge. If possible, you should add a personal note in the next-to-last paragraph so this does not appear to be a computerized letter. A scholarship brochure should be enclosed. It is important that this letter be mailed the last week of November or the first week of December, in order not to be overlooked in the donor's Christmas avalanche of mail and also to arrive before the tax year ends—unless the due date for the annual payment falls at another time during the year.

Exhibit N
Annual Letter Reminding of Pledge Payment Due

[date]
[name]
[address]

Dear [name]:

It's that time of year to remind you about your annual gift to the [fund name] Scholarship Fund.

Original pledge: $20,000
Paid to date: 12,000
Due in 1998: 4,000
Data about your scholarship:
Amount now in endowment: $12,150
1998-99 scholarship: 600

Please make your check payable either to [fund name] Scholarship Fund or University of [name] Foundation. I have enclosed a self-addressed envelope for your convenience.

I am also enclosing our 1997-98 scholarship bulletin. Your scholarship is listed on page 3. The back cover of the scholarship bulletin will show you that it now costs $[amount] for tuition and fees for an in-state student at the University of [name]; your scholarship provides significant help for a deserving student in covering this cost.

It was great seeing you and your two kids at the Homecoming coffee last month. It's hard for me to believe you have been gone from here for 15 years—until I look at the size of your children.

Let me get a jump on the season, [donor's name], and wish you and yours a happy holiday season, and a successful 1999.

Sincerely,

[name]
Dean

Encl. (college scholarship brochure and self-addressed envelope)

Exhibit O
Annual Letter Inviting Additional Gift

This annual letter serves the same purposes as the Annual Letter Reminding of Pledge Payment Due (Exhibit N), except that it is intended for donors with paid-up funds. Therefore, it suggests an add-on gift rather than a payment. A scholarship brochure should be enclosed. It is important that this be mailed no later than the last week of November or the first week of December. Again, if you can add a note in the next-to-last paragraph referring specifically to the donor, you will make this letter more effective.

Exhibit O
Annual Letter Inviting Additional Gift

[*date*]
[*name*]
[*address*]

Dear [*name*]:

It's that time of year to bring you up to date on the
[*fund name*] Scholarship Fund and give you an opportunity
to add to it before year's end, if you wish.

Your endowment now stands at: $214,507
This generates per year: $10,725

You will note on the back of the enclosed scholarship
bulletin (your scholarship is listed on page 10) the
various fees and costs of staying at the University of
[*name*] for one academic year. Tuition and fees go up as
the legislature provides less of the overall costs of
running the university. Thus, private scholarships become
even more important to help us support those outstanding
students who have financial need.

If you would like to add to your fund, the check should
be made out to the [*fund name*] Scholarship Fund or University of [*name*] Foundation. I have enclosed a self-addressed envelope for your convenience. This has beeen a
good year for the college, thanks to support such as
yours. Outstanding students attracted by scholarships like
yours have won the 1997 [*competition name*] national competition for the college again this year.

Thanks for dropping by for a visit last summer when you
were on your way to Chattanooga. Nothing gives me more
pleasure than to show off our new facilities to favorite
alumni.

Let me get a jump on the season, [*donor's name*], and
wish you and yours a happy holiday season—and a successful
1998 to all the family.

Sincerely,
[*name*]
Dean

Encl. (scholarship brochure and self-addressed envelope)

Exhibit P
Alumni Publication

Alumni publications can take the form of a newsletter or magazine. The example given here—the *communigator,* published twice a year by the College of Journalism and Communications at the University of Florida— is a hybrid of the two. These selected pages from the Spring and Fall 1996 issues show the emphasis on alumni. Note the variety of stories on alumni, with alumni notes at the bottom of each page and a coupon on one page for alumni to give the latest news about themselves. For the Spring 1996 issue alone, 160 alumni returned the coupon.

communigator

College grad programs rank high

For the ninth time in the past 13 years, University of Florida programs in journalism and communications have been ranked in the top 10 in the country.

The most recent survey, by *U.S. News & World Report* and published March 11, is a study of how academics rated graduate programs in the field.

In "The Best Graduate Schools" study, Florida is the only school with top-10 rankings in advertising, print journalism, public relations and radio/television. No school was consistently ranked first.

Treise in Toys Я Us space station (Photo by John Freeman)

The *USN&WR* rankings (top-10 only) were as follows (ties are noted with +):

Advertising

1 University of Illinois
2 University of Florida
3 Northwestern University
4 University of Texas at Austin
5 University of Georgia
6 Michigan State University
7 University of North Carolina
8 University of Tennessee
9 University of Missouri
10 Syracuse University

Print (Journalism)

1 University of Missouri
2 Columbia University
3 Northwestern University
4 University of North Carolina
5 Indiana University
6 University of Florida
7+ Ohio University
7+ University of Wisconsin
9 California-Berkeley
10 University of Kansas

Public Relations

1 University of Maryland
2 University of Florida
3 Syracuse University
4 University of Georgia
5 University of North Carolina
6 San Diego State University
7+ Ohio University
7+ University of Texas at Austin
9 Northwestern University
10 Michigan State University

Radio/Television

1 Syracuse University
2 University of Florida
3 University of Missouri
4 University of Texas at Austin
5 Northwestern University
6 Indiana University
7+ Arizona State University
7+ Columbia University
9 Ohio University
10 University of Wisconsin

For commentary on rankings, see page 3.

Debbie Treise receives record-setting $80,000 NASA research appointment

An advertising faculty member has received a joint appointment as a senior researcher in space science communication processes with NASA's Marshall Space Flight Center in Huntsville, Ala.

The $80,000 price tag makes it the largest award ever received by an individual faculty member in the College, according to **Dean Terry Hynes**. Hynes called the award to **Dr. Debbie Treise**, assistant professor of advertising, "a wonderful new plateau for the College."

Under terms of the agreement, Treise will spend three days a month at NASA and 10 weeks there in the summer. The appointment will underwrite 70 percent of her nine-month salary and 100 percent of her summer appointment.

The project grew out of an assignment last summer under the NASA Summer Faculty Fellowship Program. Treise and **Dr. Jon Morris**, associate professor of advertising, participated in the program.

Treise, who is a specialist in health communications, said she was especially interested in NASA's AIDS-related research. NASA has been conducting experiments in micro gravity protein crystal growth.

One of Treise's tasks is to help NASA communicate its scientific findings to the research community and to the media.

The NASA appointment is the largest to date for Treise, who has received some $34,000 to support other projects.

A 1974 UF graduate, she worked professionally for 15 years before earning an M.A. degree at the University of South Florida and Ph.D. degree at the University of Tennessee - Knoxville.

Her sons--Chris, 16, and Mike, 11--spent last summer with her in Huntsville. This year they'll attend Space Camp there.

This is really a good environment for them," Treise said. "Kids don't know enough about NASA." ■

Computer theft delays multimedia

by Stacy Chaulk

The theft of seven high-end computers in January has forced faculty and students in the College to improvise for the spring semester.

Plans for a new multimedia computer lab came to an abrupt halt Jan. 24 when staff discovered seven Pentium Pro computers valued at $35,000 had been stolen from a locked storage area in Weimer Hall.

Police have no suspects in the theft, which was the 32nd involving computers on campus in the last year. **Dean Terry Hynes** said the College is waiting for year-end funds from the university to replace the computers and get the lab up and running. "That's really our first hope, that we will be able to get some year-end monies from the university," she said.

Photo darkroom to become new multimedia lab (Photo by Stephanie Sinclair)

David Brumbaugh, director of the College's Information Technology Center, discovered the theft when he went to retrieve the computers from the ground floor.

He said the theft is not only a monetary loss, but a personal loss for students as well. They won't be able to do their work.

Over the Christmas break, 16 black-and-white photo enlargers were removed in anticipation of the new computer lab coming on-line.

Prof. John Freeman, who heads the photojournalism program, said the theft leaves students without the computers to run Photoshop software and having to rely on five black-and-white enlargers. "The big drawback is for the students who are caught in the middle," Freeman said. ■

Inside this issue...

High Honors
College to honor Pulitzer-winning alumnus Jim McGee. Page 3.

Private Support
Alumni and friends provide margin of excellence in 1995. Pages 6-7.

Happy Days
Ed Wells gets ready to join the ranks of the retired faculty. Pages 10-11.

Alumni Profiles
Graduates on the frontlines in Bosnia to the Atlanta Olympics. Pages 12-19.

Alumna Yvette Cardozo pictures life in Arctic igloo

Editor's Note: Yvette Cardozo, JM 1966, and her husband specialize in adventure travel. Last October they went sea kayaking with ex-headhunters in Papua New Guinea and this July they'll return to the Canadian Arctic to scuba with beluga whales. She says it is exciting, except for the hypothermia and antibiotic-resistant infections. They are winners of numerous Lowell Thomas awards for their writing and photography. They live in Issaquah, Wash. Their first-person account of an Arctic adventure follows.

by Yvette Cardozo and Bill Hirsch

When toothless old Martha handed us the raw, still warm caribou kidney, we knew it was a special event. This choice bit of fresh kill is usually reserved for the camp elder and for her to share it with us was the height of honor.

It tasted a bit like liver but with a slightly crisp snap, a hint of gamey flavor and a dense feel. And an odd thing happened. Standing there outside our igloos, dressed in our caribou skins and

Cardozo at '66 Homecoming

eating raw meat, we stopped being just observers. We were beginning to live the life ... to feel like Eskimos, or as they call themselves, Inuit.

We had journeyed up here nearly to the Arctic Circle, dead center in northern Canada, to see how the Inuit live in winter. We figured it would be the usual show where local folk play at a way of life long past...

Instead, we found a final generation of these "people of the land" living a way of life that still exists. And they were willing to share that way of life with us for several days.

It was mid-afternoon when we arrived at camp to be greeted by the Inuit who had come out earlier. Camp was nestled against a low hill on the edge of Long Lake and included a skin tent, two canvas tents, two igloos and eight dogs staked next to a bloody haunch of caribou.

The larger igloo had an entrance

> ## 'Igloos you see in cartoons aren't like the real thing.'

down three steps which led into the "kitchen" with its propane stove. Behind that, through a low tunnel, was a large room with an ice window high on the wall and a sleeping shelf that took up two thirds of the room. Caribou and Muskox hides lined the shelf and sleeping bags would go on top at night...

Igloos you see in cartoons aren't anything like the real thing. A real igloo has a third of its living space below ground and it's covered with snow to keep out wind. The visible result is a low, rubbly mound.

Ice blocks for the walls are cut from the floor of the igloo. When it's done right, the blocks just crack out whole, after which they're trimmed along the bottom and sides, fitted and tapped into place. The angled blocks are held together by mere friction.

Inside an igloo is a bit warmer than outside, but not much. We had brought a thermometer and when it was zero inside, it was zero inside. Some of us who naturally sleep cold slept VERY cold the next three nights.

The next morning after breakfast ("Indian" frybread and jam), someone spotted a caribou herd and we hustled off.

Away from camp, we were alone on a vast, white flatness, 100 miles from the nearest tree. It was like being in a small boat in the middle of the ocean. The flatness stretched to the horizon, broken only by wind ripples that looked eerily like small whitecaps.

Riding on Jacob's box sled, we raced to catch up with Silas Aittauq and his dog team, but in the few minutes we traveled, he had already done his work. Using a Remington .222 without a telescopic site, he brought down a caribou with a single shot to the neck. The animal was dead when it hit the ground. This kind of swift efficiency is necessary in a land where people grew up so poor, they bought their bullets one at a time.

Back in camp, the men skinned the animal with pocket knives, stopping every so often to tell us which part is used to make a specific piece of clothing. Upper leg is for boots, socks and mitts, the muzzle makes boot soles and the rest makes pants and parkas.

As Silas continued to skin and butcher, the animal began to look less like a hunting trophy and more like a side of beef. Except that the meat was a lot darker than beef, the result of its extremely high iron content. The red/brown was so deep, it was almost purple.

The next day, after various hikes and visits with families, we gathered in the big igloo for a demonstration of Inuit sewing and games. Mae Haqpi wore a

beaded amauti (woman's parka). Long strands of yellow, red, white and blue beads formed a fringe while leaf and gourd-like patterns covered the jacket in a rainbow swirl. That jacket had taken more than a year to make.

Martha, meanwhile, sewed a pair of mitts. She chewed the caribou hide to soften it at the edges, then stiched it together, hair side out. In the old days, the needles were bone. The thread is still sinew but these days, the women buy it on huge spindles at the Northern Store in Baker Lake.

By this time, we had spent three days in our skin clothes and they were beginning to take on a certain fragrance. It wasn't gaminess so much as essence of mealtime. The clothes were warm and soft but unbelievably bulky.

The final night, we hiked across the tundra and into the setting sun. The snow glowed pink, the ripples picking up shadows of purple and gold. Ahead, two women were backlit by the sun so that an orange glow outlined their forms. We hiked until we couldn't see even the faintest trace of camp and a deep sense of peace settled over the landscape.

For now, their world still exists but it is vanishing, fast, beneath a blanket of satellite TV dishes and jars of peanut butter.

We figured we were lucky to share this with them, even if briefly. If the object of travel is to experience other cultures on their terms, then this is the ultimate trip. ▨

---

alumni notes

advertising

James L. Martin Jr., ADV 1968, is retired owner and president of The Martin Media Group in Winter Haven. He served on the UF Advertising Advisory Council.

Stuart Shlossman, ADV 1976, is senior vice

president and associate director of the National Television & Radio Group for DDB Needham Worldwide Advertising in New York.

Charles H. Dieguez, ADV 1980, is president and owner of C.H.D. & Assoc. Inc. in Cooper City, a distributor of cardiac pacemakers and defibrillators. They also provide 24-hour monitoring services for arrhythmia detection and documentation.

Elizabeth Anne Thomas, ADV 1980, is marketing director for Transeastern Properties of South Florida Inc. in Coral Springs. She handles marketing, advertising and public relations for 34 South Florida communities built and/or developed by the company.

Katy Vorce, ADV 1983, was recently promoted from marketing manager to director

of marketing at Focus on the Family, a non-profit Christian ministry in Colorado Springs.

David Posey, ADV 1983, is a senior artist and designer at Corporate Visions in Washington, D.C. He designs for the World Wide Web and high-end multimedia graphics.

Christine Gow, ADV 1984, is a pharmaceutical sales representative for Schering Plough Pharmaceuticals in San Francisco.

Linda Peach Harmon, ADV 1984, is president and owner of a market research firm, Focus One, specializing in focus groups, in Brandon. Miss. She and her husband, an FSU alum, have two young sons.

Bruce McCoy, ADV 1984, is regional sales manager for The Papert Companies, a national newspaper rep firm, in San Francisco. Earlier he worked for J. Walter Thompson in the media department

Brian M. Lawrence, ADV 1985, is regional marketing manager for J. Walter Thompson in Chicago. He works with the Ford Motor Co. (Chicago, Cincinnati, Detroit and Pittsburgh regions). He and Gator Teresa

Sencil were recently married. He is a charter member of the Motown Gator Club in Detroit.

Ashley Rea, ADV 1985, has been promoted to vice president and management supervisor with Bates Southwest in Houston, working on Texaco Havoline brands advertising and sales promotions.

Gloria Tucker, ADV 1985, is sales manager for CBS Radio Representatives in San Francisco.

Lisa Barnett Munjack, ADV 1987, is promotion director for the New York Post in New York.

Cathleen Shawver Poor, ADV 1988, is a banking center manager for NationsBank in Melbourne.

Ken DeGilio, ADV 1990, was recently selected as executive director of the Kentucky Recreation & Park Society, a non-profit professional organization dedicated to promoting parks, recreation and tourism in Kentucky.

Ronnie London, ADV 1990, is an associate attorney with Pepper & Corazzini in Washington, D.C., specializing in broadcast law. He graduated from the Georgetown

Alumna named vice president at Fleishman-Hillard

by Liana Sucar

Pis-Dudot

Barely two years after joining the second largest independent public relations firm in the world, **Maria Lopez Pis-Dudot, ADV 1985,** was named vice president of Fleishman-Hillard in November.

Pis-Dudot (pronounced "peace-doo-dough"), who works out of the Miami/Latin America office, is responsible for developing strategies and supervising the day-to-day activities for national and international accounts.

"It's all about teamwork," said Pis-Dudot, who attributes her success to collaboration.

She works closely with clients including GEMS Television (a cable network based in Miramar) and Busch Entertainment Corporation's Florida parks (Busch Gardens and Sea World).

Before joining the St. Louis-based firm, Pis-Dudot was an account supervisor at Burson-Marsteller's Miami office. She worked on the Bacardi and AT&T accounts there.

Pis-Dudot attended UF between 1983

and 1985, after transferring from North Carolina at Greensboro.

At UF she worked for the Performing Arts Series, producing flyers, press releases, posters and other promotional materials.

"She was always delightful to work with," said Paul Newman, who was events coordinator at the time. "For two years she did a lot of great marketing and public relations for us."

Pis-Dudot also met her husband, Alejandro, at UF where he was earning a master's in accounting. He is now director of accounting at Sunglass Hut International headquarters in Miami.

They have two daughters Franchesca, Christine and a son, Alejandro. ∎

new challenges

Marilyn Little Tubb, MA 1972, has been named vice president for marketing and public relations for Shands Hospital, following the $100 million acquisition of Santa Fe Healthcare (including Alachua General Hospital) earlier this year. She had held a similar position at Santa Fe Healthcare since 1988.

Previously she was director of marketing and public relations for North Florida Regional Medical Center in Gainesville for 12 years.

She and her husband, **George F. Tubb, TEL 1967,** an attorney specializing in real estate, have a daughter.

Tubb

Bruce Binenfeld, ADV 1978, has been named director of programming at WGN-TV in Chicago. The station is available in 39 million homes outside Chicago via satellite and cable distribution.

Binenfeld came to Chicago from Boston where he held a similar position with WABU-TV. Earlier he worked as program/promotion director for WNUV-TV in Baltimore, promotion manager at KPTM in Omaha and promotion manager at WDZL-TV Miami; WBSP-TV, Ocala; WCIZ-TV, Miami; and WUSV-TV, Albany.

Binenfeld

Christy Gnann Cantrell, ADV 1979, has been promoted to vice president for marketing communications at Alfa Insurance, headquartered in Montgomery, Ala. The company offers multi-line insurance products in Alabama, Georgia and Mississippi and employs 2,000. Before joining Alfa in 1982, Cantrell was a technical writer for McDonnell-Douglas in Titusville and a retail advertising representative for the *Today* newspaper.

She and her husband, Bob, have two children--Adrienne, 11, and

Cantrell

Steven, 8. ∎

Magazine features top 1995 graduate

Elizabeth Hill, PR 1995, one of the 1995 Weimer Award winners as the top graduate in the College, was featured on the cover of the Spring 1996 issue of *Careers & Majors*, published by Oxendine Publishing Co. in Gainesville. Hill is a corporate marketing specialist in public relations and special events for Orlando Regional Medical Center (a seven-hospital group in central Florida). The magazine wrote about her experience in 1992 with EuroDisney in Paris.

The magazine's publisher and editor in chief is **W.H. "Butch" Oxendine** who also studied journalism at UF. He also publishes *Student Leader, Florida Leader* and *Returning Student* magazines and coordinates the Florida College Student of the Year Award. He has been honored as one of the top 100 entrepreneurs under 30 by the Association for Collegiate Entrepreneurs. ∎

Juskiewicz heads national fitness group

T.J. Juskiewicz, TEL 1987, was elected president of the National Association of Governor's Councils on Physical Fitness and Sports at the organization's annual meeting in Salt Lake City.

The organization was established to improve the quality of life for people in the United States through the promotion of physical fitness and healthy lifestyles.

Juskiewicz is director of the Sunshine State Games and deputy executive director of the Florida Governor's Council on Physical Fitness and Sports in Gainesville.

The Sunshine Games are scheduled for July 3-7 in Gainesville and will feature 10,000 athletes competing in 24 individual and team sports. ∎

'GATORMANIA'

A November 15 gathering of College of Journalism and Communications alumni in Jacksonville may have been the first -- but it won't be the last there or elsewhere, according to **Dean Terry Hynes.**

It will serve as a model for upcoming programs throughout Florida and the country, she said. "I look forward to meeting with groups of alumni throughout the state of Florida and the country."

The program was organized by **Diane Evans Mills,** new development director in the College, the UF National Alumni Association and a Jacksonville host group.

The buffet dinner was held at the newly renovated stadium of the Jacksonville Jaguars and attracted more than 100 alumni and friends.

The host group included **Dale Bethea, PR 1983; Ric Clarson, PR 1979; Vic**

It's great ... to be ...
a Florida communiGATOR!

DiGenti, TEL 1963; Eric Dodd, TEL 1993; C. Del Galloway, PR 1981, MA 1983; Randy Gray, PR 1979; Dawn Rodriguez Hudson, PR 1985; Joy Jarzyna, JM 1992; Nancy Schlesinger Lantinberg, PR 1992; Deborah Dalton Melnyk, ADV 1971; Stephen J. Partain, ADV 1985; Michael R. Romaner, MA 1984; Risa Waitz Schneider, ADV 1981; Gary Sease, JM 1975; Carl Smith, ADV 1989; Susan Budd Towler, PR 1985; Francine Andia Walker, PR 1981; and Gretchen Moloney White, TEL 1982.

Corporate sponsors of the gathering were the *Florida Times Union* and CSX Transportation.

And speaking of gatherings -- the 1996 Homecoming is scheduled for Oct. 11-12 in conjunction with the LSU football game. The College will host a continental breakfast in the Knight Courtyard on Saturday, Oct. 12, from 9 - 10:30 a.m.

"Mr. President and Mr. Speaker." Mr. President of the Washington, D.C., Gator Club, **Greg Williams, PR 1986,** that is (on the left). And on the right--Speaker of the House **Newt Gingrich.** Williams works for the Joint Economic Committee headed by Florida Sen. Connie Mack (R-FL), whom he formerly served as press secretary.

Lisa Buyer, PR 1989, helped create the new Gator Calling Card and related promotional materials. She is a partner (with Lisa Hoddinott) in a four-year old creative agency, L&L Communications Design Team in Deerfield Beach.

Among their pro bono clients are the Dan Marino Foundation and the Tracy Paules Memorial Softball Tournament.

The latest in the Gator license plate series is from **Nora Rendell Kovacs, TEL 1982,** who lives in Denver. She and her husband, Alex, also a UF grad, have a daughter, Victoria, who is 6.

Weimer Hall, home of the communigators since 1980 (Tom Saylor Photography)

Steve Hooper, TEL 1956, and his wife, Betty, were in high spirits awaiting Fiesta Bowl with friends in Kitchener, Ontario, Canada, where he is retired from CKCO.

Deaths

Roland H. King, ADV 1973, a painting contractor who returned to college and earned his bachelor's degree at age 54, died Dec. 11 in Hawthorne. He was 76 and an evangelist. He is survived by his wife, Jane; two sons and a daughter, two stepsons and three stepdaughters.

Jason Blocker, PR 1991, died from injuries suffered in a December 2 motorcycle accident in Nashville, Tenn. He was 27.

Effie D. Flanagan, wife of Alvin C. Flanagan and one of the College's major benefactors, died Oct. 6 in Atlanta after a long illness. She was 89.

If you don't tell us, we won't know

Alumni -- please tell us what you're doing.

Name (incl. maiden name) _____

Major/year _____ Phone (___)_____

Home address _____

City/State/Zip _____

Current Position (title/company, business address, phone -- or enclose business card) and other news.

_____

_____

_____

Deadline for fall issue is Sept. 1. Mail to *communigator*, College of Journalism and Communications, University of Florida, P.O. Box 118400, Gainesville, FL 32611-8400. Or FAX (904) 392-3919. 4-8-96

Darcy Rae Garrett, TEL 1994, is a news producer for KRIS-TV, the NBC affiliate in Corpus Christi.

Celia Bifano, TEL 1995, is an employee specialist with King Companies, a Jacksonville firm specializing in temporary staffing.

Peggy O'Leary, TEL 1995, is weekend anchor and a medical reporter for WRDW-TV in Augusta, S.C.

William J. Rourke, TEL 1995, is an advertising account executive for ADS Publisher Services in Chicago.

Dan Switzen, TEL 1995, is a technical director at CNN, Atlanta, and he adds, "the fastest person to get to this position at CNN."

director for academic support services at Florida International University in Fort Lauderdale.

Thomas H. Doerr, PR 1976, MA 1978, is news director for WPLG-TV, a Post-Newsweek station in Miami.

Diane Lenhoff Hagerman, MA 1993, is a communications specialist with the Trump Taj Mahal Casino Resort in Atlantic City. She was married to Darren Hagerman in March 1995.

Ami B. Goldberg, MA 1994, is assistant account executive with Gallaspy & Lobel Advertising in Hollywood, specializing in retail and automotive accounts, and also operates an Internet division, The CyberAd agency.

master's

Alan Jay Weiss, ADV 1971, MA 1971 is a financial adviser with schoolteachers in Santa Monica Calif., and co-author of *Financial Tips for Teachers*, now in its fifth edition.

Cynthia Cone, MA 1975, is associate

phd's

Dr. Sherry Lee Alexander, PhD 1990, is associate professor of communications at Loyola University, New Orleans.

Dr. Charles N. Davis, PhD 1995, is assistant professor in communication arts at Georgia Southern University in Statesboro.

Kaplan's 'Spicy Baloney Principle'

by E. Jack Kaplan, JM 1959

Who knew? While taking a Journalism Law final exam in 1958, I discovered the principle that would become the single most important factor in an exciting if somewhat spotty career. The question that changed my life was composed by Professor H.G. "Buddy" Davis and went something like this: "John Peter Zenger, Benjamin Franklin and Plato meet in Heaven to discuss the relationship between freedom of the press and

Kaplan

society. Describe their conversation."

Good Lord! The man was asking me to THINK!

Panic roared through every cell of my body. Half an hour later, the blue books in which we wrote our answers remained blank and mocking on the desk. A small pool of cogent thought finally seeped through the hysteria. I vaguely remembered Zenger had some connection with the first legal test of press freedom in the New Land. Franklin, of course, was the kite guy. But Plato? Of course. Plato was ... a republican! Those few facts encompassed the totality of my knowledge in this area. Why I hadn't spent more time studying for this exam is lost from memory—except the name "Joanne" keeps popping into my conscious.

Then, it happened! The EVENT. The Idea that changed my life. I began to write furiously in the blue books. Words, sentences, pages flew by. When it was over, I had managed to turn a paucity of facts into three blue books. What I had written was an EPIC POEM. Yes, it rhymed and timed. Zenger and clinger. Plato and NATO. Franklin and ... and ... Anyway I turned in the blue books and immediately began working on creative excuses for my parents as to why I had failed this course. I was also afraid that I had made

a complete fool of myself before the man I most admired, liked—yes, and even feared. Soon, the grades were posted. And there it was. Kaplan - A+. I double-checked. No mistake. Had I fooled Buddy Davis? Not possible. He knew I didn't know. I knew he knew I didn't know. He knew I knew he knew I didn't know. But he had given me the grade based on my UNIQUE, CRE-ATIVE AND NOVEL APPROACH TO THE PROBLEM. That's when it all came clear to me.

If you're going to give them baloney, you'd better make it flavorful and fun to consume. I had discovered the SPICY BAL-ONEY PRINCIPLE and it's the bedrock of all my work.

My first professional use of The Principle was tentative, but effective, in the column and feature stories I wrote for the *Atlanta Constitution*. Later, it took root and flourished in a six-year stint in advertising as creative director on RC Cola, Krystal Hamburgers and various other accounts. But The Principle did not reach full bloom until I served as a speechwriter in the White House

> *'If you're going to give them baloney, you'd better make it flavorful and fun to consume.'*

for President Jimmy Carter

Then came Hollywood. There is no more fertile—and fertilized—place for The Principle of Spicy Baloney. For me, it reached full force in writing and/or producing shows like "Laugh-In," "Designing Women" and "Hill Street Blues." There was one notable exception. I was on staff of a show called "Turn-On," which is in the Guinness Book of Records for being canceled in the shortest time on record—15 minutes into its first broadcast.

Now as a screen writer for feature films, I have taken the Spicy Baloney Principle to new heights in projects for Mel Gibson, Goldie Hawn, Alec Baldwin and others. One picture I wrote, *My Fellow Americans*, starring James Garner and Jack Lemmon, will be a Warner Brothers Christmas release this year. Modestly, I'd put it up there with the best spicy baloney I've ever written.

It is the dream of every creative person in Hollywood to win an Academy Award. Should that ever happen for me, the statue would occupy an honored position on my miniscule awards shelf. But in my house, it would not be called "Oscar." Or even the Oscar Mayer. No, in my house, the award would always be referred to with great reverence as "The Buddy." ■

Fergusons' Atlanta exhibit strikes 'Common Chords'

Bissell Ferguson Multimedia, a company headed by two UF grads, has written and produced a documentary for Atlanta's Olympic Arts Festival that has been called "first-rate" by *The New York Times*. The exhibit runs through June 1997.

Scott Ferguson, TEL 1975, and his wife, Cady Bissell, a UF film studies graduate, produced and wrote *Common Chords: The Music of the American South*, as the audiovisual element of the museum exhibition *The American South: Past, Present, Future* at the Atlanta History Museum.

Their documentary traces the journey of American Southern music from its origins in

Africa and Europe, to the fusion of many diverse influences into the globally popular sounds of the 1990s.

Among the 50 showcased performers are Eubie Blake and his ragtime piano to the Rock and Roll of Hootie and the Blowfish.

Common Chords is shown continuously via laserdisc on three monitors in the exhibit. The monitors are surrounded by rare original artifacts, including an Elvis Presley guitar and stage costume, a W.C. Handy piano, a Mother Maybelle Carter autoharp and a Louis Armstrong trumpet.

Ferguson and his wife also produced two documentaries for the new William Breman

Jewish Heritage Museum, which opened June 30 in Atlanta. They are *And None Shall Make Them Afraid*, the story of the 1958 Atlanta Temple bombing, and *The Leo Frank Case*, an exploration of the 1913 murder of a 13-year-old factory worker. The latter documentary was awarded a 1995 Cine Golden Eagle, a 1995 WorldFest Gold Award at the Houston International Film Festival and a 1995 MUSE Award, recognizing the best films, video and multimedia presentations produced for American museums.

In 1992 they researched and wrote the script for *Thurgood Marshall: A Tribute*, a film biography of the late Supreme Court Justice for the Jackie Robinson Foundation.

The Fergusons moved back to Sarasota, their hometown, from Atlanta (where they spent 15 years) in 1991, but they continue to serve many Atlanta clients. They have one daughter, Grier, who is six. ■

Patsy Cline in Southern music showcase

Fergusons with daughter Grier at exhibit

---

hit comedy

One of this fall's blockbuster films, "The First Wives Club," is directed by **Hugh Wilson, ADV 1964**, who also created the long-running TV series "*WKRP in Cincinnati*." Wilson (upper left) who was honored by the College as an alumnus of distinction in 1982, is pictured here on the set with star Bette Midler and fellow Gator **Larry Meisel, ADV 1989** (see Meisel letter to the editor on page 18 re their chance meeting). ■

Press, the Gannett newspaper in Fort Myers.

Mark Shouger, ADV 1985, is executive assistant manager (for rooms) at Hyatt Regency Tech Center in Denver.

Lori Lockshin, ADV 1986, is assistant state attorney for the Fifth Judicial Circuit in Ocala. She was recently elected chairperson of the Crimes Against Children Response Team, a program to help children in the area.

Michael A. Becker, ADV 1988, is a financial consultant for The Equitable Life Assurance Society in Hollywood. He was married in June.

Thomas C. Martin, ADV 1989, is vice president for key accounts and MIS for Miller Herman Inc., an international sales process and training company.

Daniel E. Alderman, ADV 1990, is an account executive with Williams Television Time, specializing in direct response TV.

Denise Rish, ADV 1990, is an attorney with Galvin Lowery & Meade in Chicago.

Lori Weiss, ADV 1990, is traffic manager for Hunter Hamersmith Advertising Inc. in North Miami.

Jon Adams, ADV 1991, works for Lowe

Partners, an advertising agency in New York.

Susan Berry, ADV 1991, is assistant marketing manager for Minh Food Corp. in Pasadena, Texas. She handles marketing for food service, deli and Canada.

Nicole Navarette Covar, ADV 1991, is a database director and morning show producer at WHYI/WBGG in Fort Lauderdale. Her first child, Nicholas Darren, was born March 28.

Chris Diller, ADV 1991, is manager of marketing communications for Elcotel, a Sarasota-based manufacturer of pay telephones and telecommunications systems.

Tammi Sue Hoffer, ADV 1991, is a graduate student in integrated marketing communications at Northwestern University.

Stephanie Beauchamp Kempton, ADV 1991, is advertising and public relations director for Allsup's Convenience Stores, a 300-store chain in New Mexico and West Texas. She lives in Clovis, N.M.

Scott Lukas, ADV 1991, is a senior account planner with Fallon McElligott Berlin in New York. He works on the Prudential, Diet Sprite, *The Washington Post* and NBA accounts.

Richard, ADV 1991, and Michelle Lippincott Ropp, ADV 1992, live in Oviedo, where he is territory manager for InvaCare Corp., specializing in health care in north central Florida. She is a fundraising consultant for Great American Opportunities in Orlando. They wrote, "We met in the student lounge of Weimer Hall in May 1990, were married in September 1992 and are expecting our first baby in October — and we owe it all to the College of Journalism and Communications!"

Catherine Smith-Brown, ADV 1991, is associate director of communications with United Way of Hillsborough County Inc. in Tampa.

Joel Schmitt, ADV 1992, is a proofreader and editor for Orient Graphic Arts in Omaha, Neb., working on the national and offshore K-mart account. Her first son, Damien Joseph, was born Feb. 6.

Julie Tisdale Simon, ADV 1992, is marketing coordinator for Mayor's Jewelers in Coral Gables.

Jenifyr Osborne Bedard, ADV 1993, is director of public relations and community

involvement for the American Lung Association of Southeast Florida. She and her husband, Benjamin, also a UF alumnus, were married in March 1993 and live in Palm Beach Gardens.

Kimberly Dour, ADV 1993, is production manager for Ausec & Cheney Group, an advertising and public relations agency in Tampa.

Jeff Funk, ADV 1993, is a marketing analyst for Turner Broadcasting System in Atlanta. He works with the strategic marketing group within Turner Program Services (which produces "The Lazarus Man" and the "Lauren Hutton Show" and syndicates "National Geographic," "The Flintstones," "CNN Newssource, CNN Television and other TBS entities).

Carey L. Gifford, ADV 1993, is an account executive with Trahan, Burden & Charles Inc. in Baltimore, working on the McCormick & Co. and Reading China accounts.

B.G. Payne, ADV 1993, is a database specialist with the *Chicago Tribune* after completing his master's in integrated marketing communications at Northwestern University.

Betty Sabates, ADV 1993, is an account executive with *The Miami Herald/El*

St. Paul newspaper rivalry excites editor Walker Lundy

Lundy pictured here in 1994 with Press Sunday Editor Lisanne Renner, JM 1981, who is now in Columbia University's graduate program in historic preservation (School of Architecture) and a part-time copy editor for The New York Times

During his 30-year journalism career, Walker Lundy, JM 1965, has left his mark on newspapers all over the United States. He has been editor and president of Knight-Ridder's *Saint Paul (Minn.) Pioneer Press* (circulation 270,000) since 1991.

Lundy said, "It's the best job I've ever had (other than being editor of the *Alligator*). My wife and I both love the Twin Cities, the weather aside."

After getting his start as editor of *The Alligator*, Lundy, a St. Petersburg native, worked as a reporter at the *Atlanta Journal-Constitution* and then spent nine years as executive editor of the *Tallahassee Democrat*.

He served as city editor for the *Detroit Free Press* and metro chief for the *Charlotte (N.C.) Observer*. He was managing editor at the *Fort Worth Star-Telegram* and then editor of the *Arkansas Gazette* in Little Rock.

He was a general news executive for Gannett before beginning his work at the *Pioneer Press*.

Lundy said this has been one of his favorite jobs because he enjoys life in the Twin Cities and the rivalry between the *Pioneer Press* and the *Star Tribune*, a Saint Paul edition of the Minneapolis-based newspaper published since 1987.

"It is one of the last healthy competitive markets left," Lundy said. The *Star Tribune* is half again as big as we are, but they're also half again as dumb ... so it's a fair fight. Eight years ago they declared themselves the 'Newspaper of the Twin Cities' and attempted to elbow us out of town, but they haven't

made a dent. They have 125 more people in their newsroom than we do."

The *Pioneer Press* has received several distinctions this year, including:

■ one of the nation's best-designed newspapers, according to the Society of Newspaper Design;

■ one of the top 20 Sunday sports sections;

■ one of the top five business sections; and

■ the #2 feature section.

"After 25 years, Knight-Ridder feels like home, so I expect to finish my career with them," said Lundy. "We're tired of moving."

Lundy and his wife have two children—Dan, 26, an actor in New York, and Sarah, 22, a police reporter in the Palm Beach bureau of the *Sun-Sentinel*.

Lundy said he still credits **Professor H.G. "Buddy" Davis** and **Professor John Webb** for much of his success. "I would have gotten a coveted A in Davis' class except I got the wrong time for 'Spring Fling,' and that was the year he decided to go! He gave me an F for that week."

He said Webb got him back in school after "I got kicked out for failing everything except ROTC (I got a D in that) and voted for me for editor of the *Alligator*."

He said Davis "wrote a letter to the *Alligator* alleging my election as editor was a result of campus politics, which gave me the motivation to prove him wrong."

Lundy, I; Davis 0. ■

'Old House' evolves into 'American Home' for TV's Bob Vila

Hearst Magazines has introduced a new magazine featuring **Bob Vila**, JM 1969, former host of "This Old House" on PBS. The first issue of the shelter magazine, titled *Bob Vila's American Home*, went on sale Sept. 17. Vila stars in his own series on A&E Network and is a spokesman for Sears' Craftsman tools.

He was honored by the College as an "Alumnus of Distinction" in 1989.

---

public service

Advertising chair **Dr. Joe Pisani** (third from left) was keynote speaker at the 12th annual program honoring Putnam County's top 50 high school scholars. The program is sponsored by Webb-Westbury Associates Inc., a Palatka advertising and public relations agency headed by **Dick Westbury, ADV 1958** (far left). Also pictured are (l-r) Geri Melosh, Jody Gaines and Bob Webb.

Lynn Sokler, Peter Fryefield move up

The nation's largest integrated behavioral healthcare organization has a College alumna in charge of corporate communications.

Lynn A. Sokler, PR 1974, ADV 1975, is a new vice president at Magellan Health Services Inc., with headquarters in Atlanta. The company was formerly known as Charter Medical Corp.

Sokler spent the last nine years, most recently as senior vice president, with Manning, Selvage & Lee in Atlanta, the 10th largest public relations agency in the world. She worked on the Arby's, Royal Crown and Blockbuster Corp. accounts.

Magellan is a *Fortune* 1000 corporation with 23,000 employees, providing health services in 96 facilities in the U.S. and Europe.

. . . .

Here comes another judge in the ranks of College alumni.

Peter Fryefield, ADV 1971, was appointed by Gov. Lawton Chiles to the Fourth Judicial Circuit in Jacksonville in 1995 and ran unopposed for re-election to a six-year term. He was in private

practice from 1977-95 with Margol, Fryefield & Pennington and Fryefield & Whitman, specializing in Medical malpractice. ■

Sokler

Fryefield

---

manager for Laser Institute of America in Orlando.

S. Randy Roberts, PR 1995, is an assistant account executive with Carlman, Booker, Reis Public Relations in Maitland.

Jill R. Weiner, PR 1995, is manager of economic development at the Greater Miami Chamber of Commerce. She plans seminars and meetings for Chamber committees, including the Dade Manufacturers' Council, Biomedical Exchange, Marine Industry and Marketing Committee.

Debbie Becker, PR 1996, is the marketing coordinator for Advanced Products Software Group in Naples.

Michelle Beilsmith, PR 1996, works for Turner Broadcasting in Atlanta.

Tara Brantley, PR 1996, is public relations coordinator for The Bolton Group in Dallas.

Jesse Cash, PR 1996, is an associate producer/editor at a 24-hour cable news channel in Sarasota.

Jennifer Palermo, PR 1996, is public relations coordinator for SED. a computer equipment distributor in Atlanta.

Jeff Washburn, PR 1996, is the new mall marketing director for the Lakeshore Mall in Sebring.

telecommunication

Rod Caborn, TEL 1965, joined Gilbert & Manjura Marketing as senior vice president in

January, where he specializes in new business development and public relations management. His son, a UF graduate, is now in law school.

Thomas F. Smith, TEL 1975, has been promoted to general manager and vice president of the Gulf Coast Division of POA, located in Brooksville. The firm provides outdoor advertising in Hernando, Citrus, Pasco, Pinellas, Hillsborough and Polk Counties.

Michael Ronald "Ron" O'Connnor, TEL 1976, is vice president of marketing for Farm Credit of Central Florida in Lakeland.

Gayle Rollins Davis, TEL 1977, wrote, "After 17 years in broadcasting I decided to get sane." She is now a senior technical writer with Alltel Information Services (mortgage division) in Jacksonville.

Cathy Curtis Mild, TEL 1980, is a senior account executive with WSOL-FM, WJBT-FM and WZAZ-AM in Jacksonville. She is also engaged to be married to broadcaster Jon Allen.

Leslie Berk Aron, TEL 1981, is a post production editor and producer for special projects and promotions at WTVJ-TV, the NBC owned-and-operated station in Miami. She and her husband, Benny, have a daughter, Rachel, born in March 1995.

Gary Nager, TEL 1981, has returned to Florida to become publisher and editor of two Tampa-based community newspapers, *Neighborhood News* and *Neighborhood Lifestyles*. He previously ran an advertising agency in New York.

John Hall, TEL 1983, recently built an all-

Canter's first novel a $400,000 bonanza

It's a tradition. Every journalism graduate has the dream of hitting it big someday with a first novel.

Well, one Gator just did. **Mark Canter**, JM 1982, is attending autograph parties this fall for a first novel that has already brought him $400,000 in advances.

His novel, *Ember from the Sun*, was published in England and Holland earlier this year. It will be released in the United States this fall and is scheduled for publication in Sweden, France, Japan, Germany and Spain, as well. It's also being peddled to Hollywood.

The plot? An anthropologist finds a 25,000-year-old Neanderthal woman frozen in the ice. She is pregnant with a female embryo, which he transplants into a surrogate mother. Take it from there. Canter called upon

his background as a reporter for the *Bradenton Herald* and senior editor for *Men's Health* magazine to make the scientific portions of the novel believable and exciting.

And he credited two of his professors for inculcating in him the standards of accurate research and clear writing. "Jean Chance's course in 'Fact Finding' gave me the first opportunity to do really thorough research," he said, "and I had the incredibly good luck to have a Pulitzer Prize winner, "Buddy" Davis, as a teacher in my basic reporting course."

Chance said Canter was original and unforgettable. "He is the only student I have ever had," she said, "who took an example I gave in class and ran with it to become a real participatory journalist.

He posed as a male stripper and came up with an outrageously great article for the *Alligator*."

Canter, who makes his home in Tallahassee with his wife, Margaret (an FSU graduate), and two children, is at work on his second novel, about a sudden-

ly-discovered colony of Chinese who had been living in the depths of the Amazon forests—you guessed it—hundreds of years before the arrival of Columbus to the New World.

"I guess you could call me an anthropological novelist," Canter said. ■

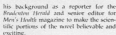

EMBER FROM THE SUN

MARK CANTER

British humor

British comedy star John Inman ("Are You Being Served?" and "Take a Letter, Mr. Jones") here with Patricia Wickham, secretary to the Dean, during a personal appearance tour at WUFT-TV. In the background are student Kristina Revell (far left) and Brent Williams, TEL 1973, MA 1985, (far right) station's development and community relations director, who coordinated the visit. (Photo by James Leslie)

fact & fiction

Dean Emeritus John Paul Jones Jr., JM 1937, is the author of a new book about Gainesville titled *What Tomorrow Brings*. It is a limited edition sequel to his earlier work, *Cold Before Morning*. The new book is described as "Gainesville's own historical novel and memoirs." Jones writes about "what citizens did in the 1920s for fun and entertainment, about the last hanging, the day the old tabernacle burned and about Gainesville's lovers' lanes." It is published by North Florida Publishing Co. in Gainesville.

Rick Tonyan, JM 1971, is the author of a "cracker western" set in frontier Florida. His first novel, from Pineapple Press, is titled *Guns of the Palmetto Plains*.

It is set in the last agonizing years of the Civil War when "rustlers and gunfighters sell their skills to the highest bidder."

Before turning to fiction Tonyan spent 17 years as a reporter for *The Orlando Sentinel*.

David Bianculli, JM 1975, MA 1977, is the author of the *Dictionary of Teleliteracy*, a book that "explores 500 programs and televised events whose impact on American culture, good or ill, will not likely be forgotten." Among the events are Army-McCarthy and Watergate hearings, John F. Kennedy's funeral, the moon landing and the O.J. Simpson trial. The book is published by Continuum Publishing.

Bianculli is the television critic of the *New York Daily News*. He was honored by the College in 1995 as an "Alumnus of Distinction."

Jim McGee, JM 1975, is the co-author of a new Simon & Schuster book about the U.S. Department of Justice, titled *Main Justice*. McGee and **Brian Duffy** take readers behind the walls of "Main Justice," which is what the department headquarters is known to insiders.

They wrote that "federal law enforcement's immense resources come at a high price—no other institution presents a more immediate threat to our freedom to live in an open society where individual liberty is protected by law."

McGee is an investigative reporter for *The Washington Post* and shared the 1987 Pulitzer Prize for reporting on the Iran-Contra Affair while at *The Miami Herald*. Duffy is investigations editor for *U.S.*

MAIN JUSTICE

News & World Report. McGee was honored earlier this year as an "Alumnus of Distinction."

Clint Johnson, PR 1975, has published his fourth book, *Touring the Carolinas' Civil War Sites*. The 380-page book covers Civil War sites in both states and details 19 car tours. It focuses on known and unmarked battlefields, historic houses and sites and the graves of famous men and women, including 54 Confederate generals. Johnson is a business writer in Winston-Salem and a longtime participant in Civil War re-enactments.

Dr. Gale A. Workman, JM 1975, MA 1978, is the author of a new book, *Partners for Excellence: Students Helping Students to Improve Journalism*, published by the Freedom Forum for Media Studies. She is professor of journalism at Florida A&M University and was an intern at CNN/Atlanta during the spring semester.

Johnson

Roxanne Kennedy Downs, TEL 1991, is a producer and programming coordinator for The Worship Network in Clearwater. She was married to Ray Downs in 1994.

Stephany Hanson, TEL 1992, is a meteorologist and reporter for KTAL-TV in Shreveport, La.

Rebecca D. Teagarden, TEL 1992, is resident director at Tulane University in New Orleans.

Kelly Thomas, TEL 1992, is print production coordinator for the Home Shopping Network in Clearwater. She and Steven Hutra, who serves in the U.S. Navy, were married on May 24.

Amy Fegebank, TEL 1993, is radio operations assistant at WMFE-FM in Orlando.

Carrie Harnish, TEL 1993, is a news producer for WESH-TV, the NBC affiliate in Orlando.

Jennifer Lopez, TEL 1993, graduated in May with a degree in meteorology from Florida State University and now works for WPTV-TV in West Palm Beach as a weather producer and fill-in meteorologist.

Eric L. Smith, TEL 1993, is director and

technical director for QVC/QZ Network in West Chester, Pa. He and Elizabeth Kipp were married in September 1995.

Raemarie Kauder, TEL 1994, works in sales and marketing for the Atlanta Motor Speedway.

Scott Kozlowski, TEL 1994, is video production coordinator at CNN Atlanta. He also produces "Cobb Prep Rally," a high school football show.

Christine Gaudiosi Seaman, TEL 1994, is assistant assignment editor with WBBH-TV and WZVN-TV in Fort Myers. Her husband, Scott, is production director for WCKT-FM.

Pascale Harrison Trotta, TEL 1994, is a freelance production assistant in Jacksonville, working on commercials and films. She and her husband, Ed, have a daughter, 6 months.

Sarah A. Walker, TEL 1994, is a news reporter for WITN-TV, the NBC affiliate in Washington, N.C.

Suzanne Boyd, TEL 1995, is a reporter for SNN, Channel 6, a 24-hour cable news channel owned by the New York Times Newspapers in Sarasota.

Ann Coccagnia, TEL 1995, is a salesperson

for The Pepsi Winner's Circle, an academic incentive program in Hollywood. She boasts, "We're Gator-owned, Gator-run and growing!"

Susannah Packing, TEL 1995, is a general assignment reporter at WYFF-TV in Greenville, S.C., a Pulitzer station.

Dan Switzen, TEL 1995, is technical director for MSNBC in Secaucus, N.J.

master's

Ray Crockett, MA 1976, is director of communications for Lockheed Martin Aeronautical Systems in Marietta, Ga.

Margaret Eves, MA 1985, is a freelance stock footage researcher in Marietta, Ga. She and her husband, Norman Andrews, are parents of a son, William, born on October 1, 1995.

Hoda Al Mutawah, MA 1987, was recently married and is moving to Oman where her husband is a magazine editor.

Susan W. Williams, JM 1972, MA 1991, has been promoted to associate in Soil and Water Science at UF where she coordinates the imple-

mentation of the Florida Homestead Assessment System, a program dealing with non-farm drinking water wells.

Carnell Moore, MA 1993, is a financial consultant with Merrill Lynch in Tampa, where he works with agents of professional athletes. Previously he headed up the Professional Sports Asset Management Group at First Union Bank's trust division in St. Petersburg.

James Lively, MA 1994, has left his position as senior account executive with Nichaus, Ryan & Haller, San Francisco, to his own firm, Lively Ideas, in Santa Rosa.

Leah Schindel, PR 1994, MA 1996, is public relations coordinator at Shands Hospitals in Gainesville. In her spare time she designs the *communigator*.

ph.d.'s

Harriet Roland, PhD 1993, received an American Society of Newspaper Editors summer professional development fellowship with the *Ann Arbor News* where she spent six weeks.